The
INFLUENCE
Effect

Peter Reeves

THE INFLUENCE EFFECT

Peter Reeves

© 2025 Peter Reeves
All rights reserved.

All rights reserved. This book or parts thereof may not be reproduced in any form, stored in any retrieval system, or transmitted in any form by any means, electronic, mechanical, photocopy, recording, or otherwise, without prior written permission of the publisher, except as provided by United States of America copyright law.

Scripture quotations are taken from the Holy Bible, English Standard Version® (ESV), copyright © 2001 by Crossway, a publishing ministry of Good News Publishers. Used by permission. All rights reserved.

Cover design by Roger Ackerman

ISBN: 9798263574895

Printed in the United States of America

For more information, visit: www.peter-reeves.com

Dedicated to the most influential people in my life and to the people I want to influence the most.

Joanna Reeves, having you as my wife is truly the greatest blessing in my life. Your presence inspires me to believe that anything is achievable. You have been a steadfast foundation in my journey, believing in me before anyone else did. Thank you for your unwavering love, especially in moments when I struggle to love myself.

I love you.

Charlie and Macklin Reeves, I love being your Dad. There's no one I want to influence more than you. I believe both of you are destined for a great future. There's nothing I would change about either of you. You make me so happy and so proud. My hope is that you take risks, invest in relationships, and build great things. You're both so special, so don't let anyone talk you out of that.

I love you.

Grace Siwale (Mom), you are easily the most influential person in my life. Your boldness changed the course of our family's history. You are the hardest-working person I know, and your drive and discipline have inspired me. Anything good I do is a testament to your influence. You not only have my respect but also deep admiration. Thank you for seeing greatness in me before I ever imagined it was possible.

I love you.

Foreword by Ryan Leak

Introduction: Build the Future You See

Preface: What I Wish Someone Told Me

SECTION ONE: The Formation of Influence

1.	Leading While Bleeding	1
2.	Legacy > Likes	10
3.	You Can't Win Alone	18
4.	If You Don't Live It, Don't Say It	26
5.	Loud Courage. Quiet Strength.	34
6.	Clarity Over Chaos	42
7.	Use What You've Got. Start Now.	50
8.	Stop Stalling. Start Stepping.	58
9.	Don't Just Build It. Own It.	64
10.	Show Up Like It Matters, Because It Does	72

SECTION TWO: The Fire of Obedience

11.	Grace Isn't Soft, It's Strong	78
12.	When God Whispers, Move	84
13.	Crisis Does not Wait, Neither Should You	92
14.	Purpose Doesn't Flinch	98
15.	Lead With Heart. Not A Mask.	104

When you finish this book, you won't just understand influence, you'll live it.

16.	Don't Fake Integrity, Build It.	110
17.	Cut Through the Noise	116
18.	See It Before They Believe It	122
19.	Create What's Missing	128
20.	Speak Like The Future Depends On It	134

SECTION THREE: The Legacy of Leadership

21.	Move Fast. Trust Deep.	140
22.	Give First. Lead Openly.	146
23.	When It's Unclear, Don't Collapse	152
24.	Don't Confuse Busy With Built	158
25.	Take The Heat. Lead Anyway.	164
26.	Your Story Is Not Just Yours	170
27.	Take The Hit. Keep Building.	176
28.	Lead When No One Claps	182
29.	Stop Motivating. Start Moving.	188
30.	Lead Like Your Lit On Fire	194

Foreword

BY *Ryan Leak*

I've known Peter Reeves for years, and I can tell you he's the real deal. He's the same man speaking to thousands from a stage as he is sitting with his family on the beach. And yes, Peter takes his family to the beach often, not as a luxury but as a deliberate way to invest in them.

One day we were on the phone, and Peter shared a verse about Jesus telling the disciples to follow a man carrying water to get ready for the Last Supper. Then he said, *"What if that was all God asked you to do? To carry water. And what if that was enough?"*

THAT LINE STOPPED ME. BECAUSE I'VE SEEN PETER LIVE IT.

He's spoken to massive crowds, yet he's just as willing to carry water, literally and figuratively. More than once, Peter has joined me at events and carried my bags, brought me water, and served without being asked. One time, a client didn't even realize he was one of the best communicators in the world. They thought he was my assistant. Peter was completely fine with that being his influence for the day. No ego. No need to set the record straight. Just faithful service in the moment God gave him.

That's why I'm so excited about *The Influence Effect*. This book is about stewarding what God has put right in front of you, whether it's leading from a platform, building a business, raising a family, or simply showing up to serve. It's about understanding that influence isn't built on titles or visibility but on faithfulness.

Peter has been someone I can recommend to my clients without hesitation because he doesn't just deliver a message. He serves the people in the room. He listens. He encourages. He leaves people better than he found them. He's challenged me personally in how I do business and how I walk with the Lord.

Influence can puff you up or it can pour you out. Peter chooses to pour himself out. And that's what makes this book so important. It will push you to look at your life through the lens of stewardship: What has God entrusted to me, and how can I use it well?

Inside these pages, you'll find real stories, timeless biblical truths, and practical steps to grow your influence every day. Peter will help you clarify what you stand for, define what you're fighting against, and live with purpose in the small and thankless things that no one sees but Heaven.

The truth is, you already have influence. The question is, what are you doing with it?

So read this book with an open heart, and then go put it into practice. Be willing to carry water when no one notices. Serve when no one claps. And trust that God sees every act of faithfulness.

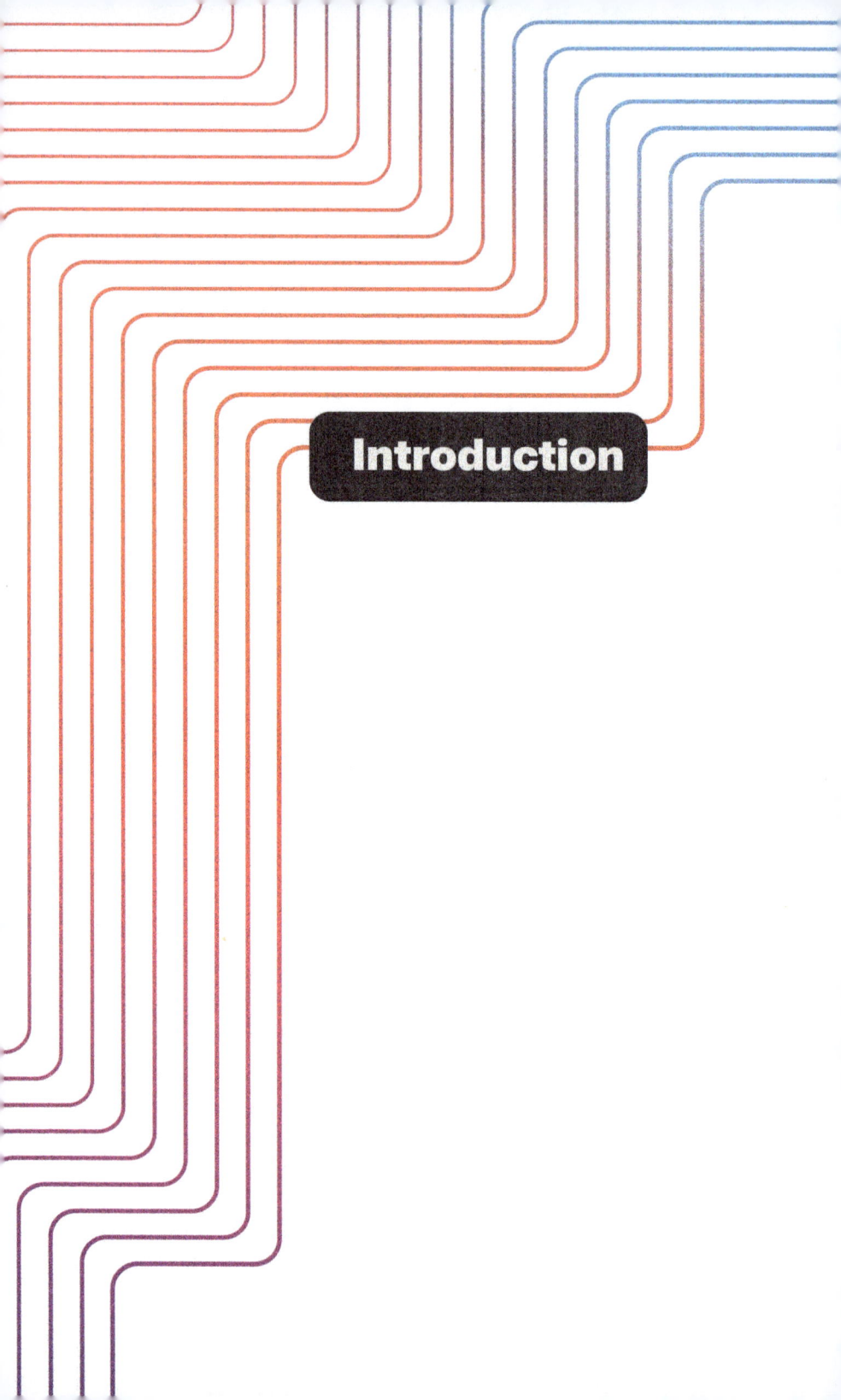

BUILDING THE
Future You See

Whether you realize it or not, you're shaping the world around you every day. Influence isn't just about titles, status, or followers, it's about how you impact people in fundamental, tangible ways. It's how you carry yourself in conversations, respond in challenging moments, and push forward when others hesitate.

Don't just read this book once and stick it on a shelf. Pick it up every day.

Influence doesn't happen overnight, you build it through daily actions, intentional decisions, and consistent discipline. When you engage with these principles, wrestle with them, and apply them, you grow your influence, not because you hold a title, but because of who you're becoming.

INFLUENCE IN EVERY SEASON

There's no better example of influence than Joseph. His life wasn't just a series of high points, he faced betrayal, injustice, and isolation. Yet, no matter where he was, he influenced his environment instead of letting his environment influence him.

- His dreams impacted his father's house, even though they made others uncomfortable.

- In Potiphar's house, his integrity gained him influence, notwithstanding his position as a servant.

- In prison, he led through service, not position. He interpreted dreams, helped others, and built trust.

- In Pharaoh's palace, he saved an entire nation because of his wisdom and preparation.

At no point did Joseph complain, blame God, or wait for a better opportunity. He didn't need a title to influence, he lived with conviction.

That's the heartbeat of this book: you can only influence when you have something to stand on.

THE ENEMIES YOU MUST CREATE

Most people think influence is about winning people over. It's not. Real impact comes from defining what you're fighting against. Not people, but problems.

- Complacency is an enemy.

- Toxic culture is an enemy.

- Lack of vision is an enemy.

The best teams, organizations, and movements don't form just because people want to "do good." They form because people identify an obstacle and commit to destroying it. They rally around a common enemy and choose to fight together. If you don't define the battle, you can't build momentum.

This book will help you identify the battles that matter, rally people around them, and create lasting forward movement.

HOW THIS BOOK WORKS

I don't write fluff. I based this book on actionable principles, ones I pull directly from scripture, real life leadership, and the habits of other great influencers.

John Maxwell once said, "Leadership is influence, nothing more, nothing less." But most people miss the truth behind that line: influence doesn't sit back. It demands intention. It demands conviction. And most of all, it demands action.

You don't increase influence by accident. You increase it by being deliberate.

THE FUTURE YOU SEE

Great influencers don't just react to the present, they create a vision of the future and pull people toward it. What future do you see?

As you work through this book, I challenge you to:

1. Engage with these ideas daily. Influence isn't a one time decision, it's a habit. Touch this book every day.
2. Clarify your convictions. Your influence will be shallow if you don't know what you stand for.
3. Define your enemies. What needs to change? What problems are you willing to take on?
4. Move toward the future you see. Influence moves forward, not backward.

When you finish this book, you won't just understand influence, you'll live it.

LET'S GET *TO WORK.*

Preface

WHAT I *Wish Someone* TOLD ME

"Peter, don't just work on what you do, work on who you're becoming. Let your work flow out of who you are." A man once spoke those words to me, a man whose quiet strength carried deep wisdom. He didn't speak often, but when he did, his words carried weight. For over 30 years, he faithfully served our church as a deacon, trustee, Sunday school teacher, and even bus driver.

He didn't just leave a legacy in our church; he left one in our city. His steady faith and servant's heart impacted lives well beyond the pews. He never rushed into conversations or flooded you with advice, but when he opened his mouth, people listened. His voice held a kind of authority that only comes from a life rooted in God. I remember the day he pulled me aside, looked me in the eye, and asked, "Peter, what do you want to do with your life?" His question didn't catch me off guard. I had carried the answer for years, maybe even since childhood. I looked at him and said, without hesitation, "I want to impact the world for Jesus."

I didn't have to search for the words. That purpose had always lived in my heart.

Growing up in a single-parent home without my dad, I wrestled with questions about where I belonged and how I'd rise above the odds. My future felt uncertain. But one thing remained clear: I knew I was called to lead. I didn't know what form it would take, but I felt the weight of that calling deep in my soul. Still, even with that clarity, I saw a gap, a space between who I was and who I wanted to become. I constantly asked myself a simple yet life-shaping question: How do I become the leader God has called me to be?

Leadership doesn't happen in a moment. It's not something you master once and for all. As Simon Sinek put it, "No one is a master leader." The best leaders never stop learning, evolving, and growing. And while you can't master leadership, you can develop it. Over time, I've realized leadership development is more than learning new strategies or sharpening your skills. It's about becoming someone God can trust to lead others. Because when I look around at the world, one thing stands out: nothing remarkable happens by accident.

Every great movement, every extraordinary accomplishment, is the result of a leader who dared to cast a vision, assemble a team, and move forward with boldness and determination. Greatness is never an accident. It results from intentionality, discipline, and faith. That's why I wrote this book. My goal is to teach you about leadership and help you become the leader God has called you to be.

Leadership starts with who you are, not just what you do. As you deepen your relationship with God, your leadership will naturally grow alongside it. I designed this book to meet you right where faith and leadership intersect. You don't have to choose between spiritual growth and leadership development, you can pursue both. The most effective leaders lead from a deep well of faith.

Inside these pages, you'll explore timeless biblical truths woven together with practical leadership principles. I'll challenge you to reflect on your journey, examine your heart, and take bold, intentional steps toward becoming a better leader. But don't just read this book, engage with it. Highlight what hits home. Underline what stretches you. Bookmark what you'll want to revisit. Take time to reflect, answer the questions, and step into the challenges. Leadership isn't a spectator sport; it demands your daily commitment to grow, learn, and lead with purpose. If you show up and commit to this process, I believe this book will transform your leadership and your life. It will draw you closer to God, sharpen your skills, and equip you to make a lasting impact in your family, your workplace, your church, and wherever God leads you next.

This is not just a book about leadership, it's a guide to becoming the leader God has called you to be. It's a roadmap for living out your purpose, fulfilling your potential, and leading with faith, courage, and conviction. So, as we begin this journey together, I want to challenge you to approach this book with an open heart and an open mind. Be willing to wrestle with the hard questions, step out of your comfort zone, and embrace the growth process. The world desperately needs leaders willing to rise to the occasion, leaders who lead not from a place of power or ambition but from a place of purpose and faith.

I believe you're one of those leaders.

The question is: Are you ready to step into the calling God has placed on your life?

LET'S *GET STARTED.*

Chapter 1

LEADING *While* BLEEDING

I still remember sitting across from him in that office. He didn't speak with malice, but every word hit like a door closing. "You're not qualified for this," he said, almost like he needed to get the disclaimer out before I could even start. "This is temporary. Just don't mess anything up." He didn't welcome me, he tolerated me. He didn't want me there, and he didn't hide it. He only brought me on because the previous youth pastor left suddenly, and no one else stepped up.

I wasn't his first pick, second, or third. I was the only option left, and he made sure I knew that from day one. I walked out of that office carrying a strange mix of excitement and uncertainty. I finally had my first chance to lead in ministry, something I had dreamed about since I was a kid. But I also knew I had stepped into a situation where my leader didn't believe in me. If something went right, he claimed the credit. If anything went wrong, he made sure I took the blame. And he didn't keep that opinion private, he told the rest of the staff exactly how he felt about me.

For months, I showed up to an environment that exposed every flaw. Every time I made a mistake, or even made a decision that looked different from his, he called it out, sometimes in front of the entire team. He didn't encourage me. He didn't affirm me. He didn't trust me. He didn't try to develop me, he just endured me. And yet, I loved it. Not the doubt. Not the lack of support. But the work itself. I loved standing in front of students. I loved pouring into the leaders. I loved preaching, praying, and counseling.

Those moments reminded me why I said yes in the first place. I didn't show up to prove anything to him, I showed up because I knew I was walking in my calling. That season stretched me. It exhausted me. It exposed my insecurities. But it also made me stronger. Leading under someone who didn't believe in me built a resilience I didn't know I needed. It forced me to trust God's approval over man's validation. And it taught me something

I now carry everywhere I go: Leadership isn't about waiting for ideal conditions, it's about showing up anyway, especially when the odds are against you.

SCRIPTURE FOCUS:
2 CHRONICLES 15:16–19 ESV

'Even Maacah, his mother, King Asa removed from being queen mother because she had made a detestable image for Asherah. Asa cut down her image, crushed it, and burned it at the brook Kidron. But the high places were not taken out of Israel. Nevertheless, the heart of Asa was wholly true all his days. And he brought into the house of God the sacred gifts of his father and his own sacred gifts, silver, and gold, and vessels. And there was no more war until the thirty-fifth year of the reign of Asa.'

I learned something in my Kidron Valley season that has stuck with me ever since: hard times are one of the greatest tools for creating strong leaders. See, the Kidron Valley is a significant geographical and spiritual location in the Bible, appearing in both the Old and New Testaments. It is a deep ravine that runs between Jerusalem and the Mount of Olives, serving as a natural boundary to the east of the city. It is in this valley that King Asa makes difficult decisions in the face of adversity. The truth is, you don't become great by leading when it's easy. You become great by leading when it's hard, when no one is applauding, when you feel like you're the only one who sees the vision. If you can keep moving forward in that kind of season, nothing can break you when your time comes.

If you lead in a difficult situation under a boss who doubts you, in a place where you feel unseen, in a role where the weight feels heavy and the support feels light, lean in. Use it. Build resilience in the fire. Step into the pressure. Let it shape you. This is where real leaders rise.

1. LEADERS MAKE TOUGH CALLS.

The Kidron Valley is a place of decision, either for repentance, cleansing, or judgment. Let's be honest, making hard decisions is never easy. Ignoring problems, avoiding confrontation, or keeping everyone happy is much easier. But is it the best idea? We see this in 2 Chronicles chapter 15 when King Asa didn't back down, even when it meant removing his mother from leadership. Why? Because the right choice outweighed the easy option.

- Leadership is problematic because it requires courage.
- Sometimes, you'll have to stand up to friends, family, or even your doubts.
- Challenging does not automatically mean bad. As a leader, you must understand that helpful and challenging can exist simultaneously.

2. YOUR VALUES > YOUR FEELINGS

Feelings are unpredictable, they can change with a text, a look, or even a rough moment. But Asa didn't let his feelings guide his decision. His values, honoring God and doing what was right, ultimately led the way.

- Feelings say: "I don't want to hurt anyone."
- Values say: "This matters too much to ignore."
- Leaders don't act based on how they feel in the moment but on what they believe matters most in the long run.

3. DON'T ASSUME EVERYONE IS OK, DIG IN.

Have you ever found out a friend was struggling and realized no one bothered to ask? King Asa didn't wait around or make assumptions, he paid attention, spotted the problem, and acted. Great leaders don't overlook people, they care for them. When you lead, show your team they're not just there to complete a task. Make it clear: they carry value, and they play a vital role in the mission you're building together.

- Leaders ask the hard questions.
- Leaders don't ignore small cracks in relationships, teams, or their hearts.
- Moments of uncomfortability often translate into moments of vulnerability and growth.

Being a leader means caring enough to dig into the details, even when it's uncomfortable.

4. MOVE FROM INTENTION TO ACTION

Good intentions don't change anything. Asa didn't just talk about fixing the problem, he acted. Leadership means stepping out and making it happen.

- You say you want to lead better. Start serving somewhere.
- You say you'll work on your relationship with God. Set a plan to pray daily.

When you procrastinate, you send a clear message: the task doesn't matter enough to you right now.

Action is the gap between where you are and where you want to be.

5. LOYALTY TO GOD OVER POPULARITY

King Asa could've taken the easy route, he could have ignored his mom's actions to keep the peace. But Asa stayed loyal to God instead. For you today, loyalty to God might look like this:

- Turning down opportunities that compromise your faith.
- Standing up for what's right when everyone else is silent.
- Making choices that honor God, not just impress people.

Influence fades, popularity shifts. But God's approval lasts forever.

6. LEADERSHIP BRINGS PEACE

At the end of the story, Asa's leadership brought peace to the land. Not because he avoided conflict but because he led with clarity and conviction.

The Hebrew word for peace is Shalom, a verb that means to arrive at a state of peace. Action is required. Shalom refers to restoring broken peace. Hence, real peace isn't just the absence of turmoil. It's knowing you honored God and did the right thing, even when it was hard.

- Peace happens when you lead with integrity.
- Peace follows bold obedience to God.
- Peace requires cultivation.

CLOSING THOUGHT:

Leadership is influence, whether leading your friends, family, a small group, or a team at work. Influence is a gift God has entrusted to you. Lead boldly. Make the tough decisions. Choose values over feelings. And bring God's peace wherever you go.

PRAYER FOR LEADERS:

"God, give me the courage to make tough calls, the wisdom to act on my values, and the strength to stay loyal to You above all else. Help me bring peace through my leadership. Amen."

The Effect

- Is there a tough decision you're avoiding? How can you step into it with courage and faith?

- Take 5 minutes today to write down your values. What do you stand for, no matter the cost? What are your nonnegotiables?

- Who in your life could use a check in? Send a text, call, or ask them, "Hey, how are you doing?"

- What's one thing you need to act on this week? Stop putting it off and take the first step.

- Are you living for applause from people or faithfulness to God?

- What would it look like to lead in a way that brings peace to your friendships, family, or team?

The **INFLUENCE** *Effect*

Chapter 2

LEGACY > *Likes*

I didn't know what I was stepping into when I first started apprenticing under him. I knew he was one of the best speakers I'd ever seen, and somehow, I'd ended up with a front-row seat to watch how he did it. From the start, it was clear that he wasn't just interested in delivering great messages, he was passionate about leaving something behind that would last longer than his time on stage.

The **INFLUENCE** *Effect*

He always dragged me along on trips, taking me to conferences and events where he was the keynote. I wasn't just tagging along to carry bags, I was there to learn how to lead and communicate. I thought I was just observing, but he always had more in mind.

Once, he had the most significant opportunity of his career, the crowd most people spend a lifetime dreaming of. He had spent weeks preparing, and when the day came, he looked over at me and said, "I want you to open for me." I couldn't believe it. Here he was, with the largest audience he'd ever had, and he wanted to share the platform with me. He wasn't worried about me overshadowing him or about me tanking the moment. He just wanted to give me a shot.

That's when I realized the kind of leader he was, he didn't just want to be known as a great speaker. He wanted to be known for raising up other great speakers. He didn't hoard opportunities, he handed them out like candy. It wasn't just about his moment but about investing in the next generation of communicators.

When we traveled, we would spend countless hours crafting messages, not just his, but mine. Sometimes we'd work on talks I'd never even give. I'd be exhausted, mentally fried from going over the same point again and again, but he'd just keep pushing. He'd challenge me to dig deeper, to make every word count, and to talk about what I loved.

He used to say, "If you're not talking about what you love, you're just making noise." That's probably the most important lesson I ever learned from him, talk about what you love, and talk about it a lot.

He wasn't afraid of me bombing on stage, either. He almost seemed to expect it. He knew that failure was a better teacher than success could ever be. Once, he asked me to speak at an event, and I knew I wasn't ready. He knew it too. But he wasn't worried about it. He just wanted me to take the risk and learn from the experience. He saw potential where I just saw fear.

There was another time when he caught me off guard. We were at an event, and he went on stage to introduce himself. After his intro, he looked at the crowd and said, "Actually, I'm gonna bring my mentee up here to speak." I wasn't prepared. Not even a little. But that day I learned something else: Always have a talk ready. You never know when the opportunity will come; if you're not prepared, you'll miss it.

> *Let your yes be yes and your no be no. Anything in between invites confusion, unreliability, and doesn't add to your leadership or legacy.*

He taught me that you're only as impactful as the legacy you leave behind. His legacy wasn't just about his success, it was about how many people he helped succeed. It was never about him staying on top but how many others he could lift along the way.

Looking back, I realize that he didn't just teach me how to communicate, he taught me how to lead with legacy in mind. He knew his influence wouldn't last unless he passed it on. That's how I want to lead, not just looking for my opportunities but creating them for others.

If there's one thing I learned from him, it's this: You're not a leader until you raise up other leaders. It's not about holding the spotlight but pointing it at the next person in line. That's how you build something that lasts. That's how you leave a legacy worth remembering.

In this scripture, the psalmist highlights how David embraced this principle, showing his focus on leaving a legacy that would outlive him.

> SCRIPTURE FOCUS: PSALM 132:1–5
>
> *"Lord, remember David and all the hardships he endured. He swore an oath to the Lord; he made a vow to the Mighty One of Jacob: 'I will not enter my house or go to my bed, I will allow no sleep to my eyes or slumber to my eyelids, till I find a place for the Lord, a dwelling for the Mighty One of Jacob.'"*

1. HONORING THOSE WHO CAME BEFORE YOU

The psalm begins with a call to "remember David," a leader who sacrificed, endured hardships, and lived with a heart entirely devoted to God. David's example reminds us that authentic leadership doesn't start with us. We stand on the sacrifices and faithfulness of those who came before us:

- Parents who prayed for us.
- Mentors who invested in us.
- Leaders in Scripture who showed us how to follow God faithfully.

Leadership means humility, recognizing that you didn't get here alone. It's about honoring legacy while carrying the mission forward.

2. FOCUSING ON BUILDING FOR GOD, NOT FOR YOURSELF

Are you more focused on building for yourself or God?

David's focus wasn't on building his legacy but on creating a place where God's presence could dwell. In a world obsessed with likes, followers, and achievements, Godly leadership flips the script:

- It's not about your platform but God's kingdom.
- It's not about being seen, it's about making God known.

True leaders use their influence to allow God to move in their lives, relationships, and communities.

3. MAKING PUBLIC COMMITMENTS THAT YOU STICK TO

David swore an oath to the Lord and followed through. Public commitments are robust because they:

- Build accountability.
- Show others you're serious.
- Strengthen your resolve to stick to what you've promised.

It's easy to make commitments, posting goals, promising change, or saying, "I'll pray for you." The real test of leadership is whether or not you follow through. What commitments have you made to God or others that you must follow through on?

- Starting that Bible reading plan?
- Serving consistently at church?
- Being there for a friend who's struggling?

Let your yes be yes and your no be no. Anything in between invites confusion, unreliability, and doesn't add to your leadership or legacy.

4. CHOOSING WORK ETHIC OVER COMFORT

David said, "I will not enter my house or go to my bed… till I find a place for the Lord." Purpose and urgency drove David's leadership. As a result, his focus was not on what was convenient or comfortable.

Leaders today face the same choice:

- Do you prioritize what's easy or what matters?
- Do you take shortcuts or work hard to honor God and serve others?

Leadership requires grit. There will be seasons where you'll need to sacrifice comfort, sleep, time, energy, to pursue what God's calling you to build.

CLOSING THOUGHT:

Psalm 132 reminds us that leadership is more significant than us. It's about honoring the legacy of faith, building for God's glory, keeping our commitments, and working hard, even when difficult. God is looking for young and old leaders who say, like David, "I won't stop until I build something for You."

PRAYER FOR LEADERS:

"God, thank You for the leaders who came before me. Help me honor their legacy while building for Your glory. Please give me the strength to keep my commitments and work hard, even when it is uncomfortable. May my leadership make space for Your presence to dwell. Amen."

The Effect

- Who in your life paved the way for you spiritually or as a leader? Take time this week to thank them, pray for them, or reflect on their example.

- Ask yourself: "How can I build something that points others to God this week?"

- Write down one commitment you've made (or need to make) and take a step to follow through today.

- Ask yourself, "What's one area in my life where I need to improve my work ethic?" Whether it's your faith, school, job, or serving, lean into hard work for God's glory.

Chapter 3

YOU Can't Win ALONE

I used to believe that if I worked hard enough, stayed focused, and kept my head down, I could do ministry, leadership, and calling, on my own. I didn't want to ask for help. I didn't want to need anyone. Part of that came from pride. But honestly? A lot of it came from pain. I was the first in my family to pursue becoming a pastor. And when I told my dad that's what I wanted to do, he laughed. Not in a cruel way, more like someone hearing a joke they didn't expect. The moment stuck with me.

The **INFLUENCE** *Effect*

Meanwhile, I looked around and saw other young leaders my age being celebrated, cheered on, and pushed forward by dads who had walked that road before them. I couldn't help but think, "Why not me?" I loved God. God had called me. But I felt like I was walking into it entirely alone. Then one day, my youth pastor looked me in the eye and said something I'll never forget:

"God is going to do something through you that hasn't been seen in your family before." That moment broke something in me. Not just the disappointment, but the idea that I had to carry this all by myself.

I didn't know it then, but God was already surrounding me with the kind of people I didn't even know I needed. Sam, an evangelist, invited me to travel with him in college. I thought I would just help set up sound and carry bags. But Sam didn't see me as a helper, he saw me as a leader in development. Through him, I learned how to trust God in real time, depend on Him in unfamiliar places, and let go of needing to have it all figured out.

> *Progress, not perfection, should be the goal.*

Then came Jacob, who took me under his wing and taught me how to communicate. Not just how to deliver a message, but how to craft one. He taught me that preaching wasn't a performance but a sacred art form. He didn't just show me how to speak. He showed me how to say something that mattered. And then there was Josh. The guy who sees potential before the rest of the room does. Josh believed in me when my résumé was still just faith and fire. He spoke my name in rooms I didn't have access to. He gave me credibility by association, and I'll never forget that. These men didn't have to help me. They didn't owe me anything. But they saw me, believed in me, and walked with me.

And here's what I've come to know deep in my bones: nobody becomes who they're supposed to be alone. Jesus modeled this from the very beginning. He built a team. He poured into them. He traveled with them. He washed their feet. He corrected them, fed them, sent them out, and brought them back again. He didn't do it all by Himself, He chose to lead with others. Because now I know better. The myth of doing it alone? It's just that, a myth.

> **SCRIPTURE FOCUS: ACTS 4:32–37**
>
> *All the believers were one in heart and mind. No one claimed their possessions were theirs, but they shared everything they had… Joseph, a Levite from Cyprus, whom the apostles called Barnabas ('son of encouragement'), sold a field he owned, brought the money, and put it at the apostles' feet.*

1. PURSUING UNITY AMONG THE TEAM

Acts 4 describes a group of believers who were "one in heart and mind." That kind of unity doesn't just happen, it's built. Leadership means working to bring people together and not allowing competition, ego, or division to win.

Are you helping your team (friends, family, ministry, or workplace) stay unified, or are you letting little disagreements or pride cause division?

Scriptural truth says that:

- **Unity happens when we put the mission over our agenda.**
- **Unity requires humility, valuing others' contributions as much as our own.**

Leaders don't stand on the path of greatness alone; they are lifted there by the teams of people who helped them build their legacy.

2. BEING GENEROUS

The believers in Acts shared everything they had because they knew it wasn't theirs to begin with, it was God's. Generosity is a mark of great leaders because it shows they trust God as their provider.

Generosity can look like:

- **Sharing your resources (money, time, skills).**
- **Helping someone out even when it's inconvenient.**
- **Living open handedly, not holding too tightly to what you have.**

Generous leaders build a culture of giving that impacts everyone around them.

3. STRIVING TO BE MORE LIKE JESUS

The believers' actions reflected Jesus's heart, generous, selfless, and focused on others.

Leadership isn't about being perfect; it's about looking more like Him daily.

Progress, not perfection, should be the goal.

Ask yourself:

- **Am I leading with love, humility, and truth?**
- **Are my actions pointing others to Jesus or myself?**

Being like Jesus isn't just about what you say, it's about how you live, lead, and love others.

4. CARING ABOUT THOSE IN NEED

In Acts, the believers ensured "there were no needy persons among them." They paid attention to the struggles of people in their community and did something about it. Leadership means having eyes to see and a heart to respond.

- **Look around: Who's struggling? Who's being overlooked?**
- **Leaders act, they don't just say, "I'll pray for you." They ask, "How can I help?"**

Are you leading with compassion and actively helping those in need?

5. NOT TRYING TO BECOME KNOWN BUT ALLOWING THE TEAM TO BE KNOWN

Barnabas (Joseph) sold a field and gave the money without needing the spotlight. Instead of making himself the hero, he encouraged the whole community to thrive.

Authentic leadership isn't about being the star but helping the team succeed.

- Leaders elevate others instead of seeking attention.
- Leaders care more about 'we' than 'me'.

When you let go of the need to be seen, you create space for something bigger, God's work in and through the team.

Do you care more about getting credit or about the team winning together?

CLOSING THOUGHT: LEAD LIKE BARNABAS

Acts 4 shows us a beautiful picture of leadership: unity, generosity, humility, and compassion. Barnabas didn't lead for his gain, he led to encourage others and build God's kingdom. What if your leadership looked like that?

PRAYER FOR LEADERS:

"God, help me surrender my ego, agenda, and plan. As I strive to lead with unity, generosity, and humility, interrupt me so that I may see those in need. Amen."

The Effect

- Reach out to someone on your team or your circle today and encourage them. Let them know you're with them and for them.

- What's one way you can practice generosity this week? Maybe it's paying for someone's lunch, donating your time, or sharing something you own.

- Spend 10 minutes reflecting or journaling: "How can I lead like Jesus in my family, friendships, or work this week?"

- This week, take a step to care for someone hurting. Maybe it's offering help, listening to their story, or meeting a practical need.

- This week, celebrate someone else's contribution. Give credit publicly and make sure they know how valuable they are.

Chapter 4

IF YOU *Don't Live It,* DON'T SAY IT.

I remember dreading math. It wasn't just a struggle, it was an all-out battle. Numbers didn't just confuse me; they frustrated me. That's when I got a math tutor. She wasn't just some college kid picking up side work. She was in the middle of earning her master's degree,

The **INFLUENCE** *Effect*

balancing a heavy course load of her own while trying to help me make sense of equations and formulas. One thing that set her apart right away was how much she cared about the process of learning, not just the grade. She didn't just want me to pass the exam, she wanted me to actually know the material. She'd say things like, "It's not about getting through this assignment, it's about understanding why it works this way. That's what will help you later on."

One day, I was hunched over my math homework, grinding through another set of problems she'd given me, and I noticed something. Across the table, she was working on her master's coursework too. I realized that what she preached to me wasn't just theory. She was living it. She was stressed, tired, and probably overwhelmed, but she never cut corners. If she expected me to dig in and really learn the material, she was doing the exact same thing on her end.

That's when it clicked: what she said was echoed by what she did. She didn't just talk about dedication, she modeled it. She didn't just tell me that understanding was important, she practiced it by mastering her own field of study. I learned that leading by example isn't just about saying the right things. It's about living them out so people can see consistency between your words and actions.

One day, after working through a particularly tough problem, she asked me a simple question:

"What makes a great student?"

I thought about it for a second and said, "Dedication, consistency, and understanding."

She nodded, but then took it further. We spent the next 45 minutes unpacking those words. She pushed me to think deeper about how to put those qualities into practice. We discussed how knowing what to do and doing it are two different things. She explained that understanding is just the first step, being able to teach it to someone else is when you know you've got it.

That conversation stuck with me. It wasn't just about math, it was about life. She showed me that follow-through matters, that it's not enough just to have knowledge, you must apply it. And she didn't just say it; she proved it by how she lived, studied, and worked tirelessly at both her own goals and mine.

> *True leaders protect the mission, even when it's uncomfortable.*

She taught me more than math; she taught me a mindset. Leading by example means consistently showing up, putting in the work, and letting your actions match your words. Too many people know how to say the right things, but don't back it up with their lives. She wasn't like that. She showed me that you must live out what you're trying to teach in order to influence others.

Jesus teaches the disciples a similar lesson in Matthew 23:1–5

> Then Jesus said to the crowds and his disciples: 'The teachers of the law and the Pharisees sit in Moses' seat. So you must be careful to do everything they tell you. But do not do what they do, for they do not practice

what they preach... Everything they do is done for people to see.

Jesus warned the crowds and his disciples of the double life the Pharisees lived. Conversely, my tutor taught me more than any textbook ever could. It made me realize that real leaders don't just talk about dedication, they live it. They don't just tell people to push through, they're pushing too. That's the kind of leader I want to be. Someone who doesn't just say it, someone who lives it.

1. TEACHING PEOPLE HOW TO THINK

Jesus called out the Pharisees for imposing rules instead of teaching people to think and live wisely. Leaders don't just give commands, they help people grow in discernment.

- Leadership is about guiding people to think critically, biblically, and wisely.
- It's about showing why something matters, not just what to do.

A good leader doesn't create followers, **they create thinkers and future leaders.**

2. WARNING PEOPLE ABOUT POTENTIAL DANGERS TO THEIR MISSION

Jesus warned the people to watch out for the Pharisees' hypocrisy, which distracted them from living their true mission. Leaders are called to do the same:

- Speak up when you see someone drifting off course.

- Challenge the things (habits, attitudes, distractions) that could sabotage someone's potential.

True leaders protect the mission, even when it's uncomfortable.

3. MAKING SURE YOUR WORDS MATCH YOUR ACTIONS

Jesus' biggest critique of the Pharisees was their hypocrisy, they said the right things but lived the wrong way. As leaders, our credibility comes from integrity.

- Words without actions = hypocrisy.
- Actions without words = confusion.
- Words and actions aligned = influence.

Takeaway: People don't follow what you say, they follow what you show.

4. HELPING OTHERS BECOME THE BEST VERSION OF THEMSELVES

The Pharisees weighed people down with burdens, but Jesus came to lift them up. Great leaders don't crush others with expectations, they empower them to grow into who God created them to be.

How do you help others thrive?

- Encourage them when they doubt themselves.
- Challenge them to step into their gifts.
- Celebrate their wins, big and small.

Leadership is about helping people discover and live out their God-given potential.

CLOSING THOUGHT: LEAD LIKE JESUS, NOT THE PHARISEES

Jesus didn't just talk about leadership, He lived it. He taught truthfully, warned with love, led by example, and empowered others to become their best selves. The Pharisees? They made leadership about appearances and self-promotion. Let's choose to lead like Jesus instead.

PRAYER FOR LEADERS:

"God, help me lead with integrity, guiding others to think wisely and live boldly for You. Give me the courage to warn those drifting off course and the humility to live out what I teach. Help me empower others to become who You created them to be. Amen."

The Effect

- **Who looks up to you (friends, siblings, teammates)? This week, have a meaningful conversation to guide them toward wisdom, not just quick answers.**

- **Are you bold enough to lovingly call out dangers that might hold someone back from fulfilling their purpose?**

- **Who in your circle needs a loving warning about something pulling them off track? Pray about it, then speak with kindness and truth.**

- **Choose one area where your actions must catch up with your words (serving, integrity, prayer, work ethic). Take one step to close that gap this week.**

- **Is there a gap between what you say and what you do? Are you living the life you're encouraging others to live?**

- **Who can you encourage or challenge this week to step into something more significant? Send a text, write a note, or grab coffee with someone who needs to be reminded of their value and potential. Speak life into them.**

Chapter 5

LOUD COURAGE.
Quiet Strength.

He never said it out loud, but I knew Josiah wanted to be seen. Not in a desperate way, he just had that natural pull. He was sharp. Creative. Had rhythm in his hands and fire in his game. If he wanted it, popularity would've been easy.

But something shifted after he gave his life to Jesus. It wasn't a big, dramatic moment, no neon sign or spotlight.

It all started with a simple pause before lunch.

In the middle of a packed cafeteria or breakroom, he'd stop, bow his head, and whisper a short prayer over his food. At first, no one noticed. Then they did. And they started leaving, one by one. People who used to laugh with him, sit by him, invite him into everything, were gone. Some moved out of discomfort, others out of mockery. They didn't get it. Honestly, at first, although I was his pastor, neither was I, so I asked him how he felt about it. He looked up, calm as ever, and said, "I miss them sometimes. But weirdly, I've never felt closer to God." No bitterness. No need to defend himself. Just this quiet strength in his eyes.

> *Leadership isn't found in who follows you—it's in who you refuse to stop being, even when they don't.*

Here's what wrecked me: he didn't push back or go cold. He bought lunch for the same people who mocked him. What kind of 17-year-old does that? Who shows that kind of grace when everyone else walks away? He still brought the same energy to school, practice, and every room he walked into.

But the applause didn't matter anymore. He wasn't chasing attention, he was becoming someone solid. Not loud. Just real.

He taught me something I haven't forgotten since: Leadership isn't found in who follows you, it's in who you refuse to stop being, even when they don't.

SCRIPTURE FOCUS: DANIEL 4:24–27

Therefore, Your Majesty, be pleased to accept my advice: Renounce your sins by doing what is right and your wickedness by being kind to the oppressed. It may be that then your prosperity will continue.

1. SPEAKING UP EVEN WHEN IT'S UNCOMFORTABLE

Daniel stood before King Nebuchadnezzar, one of his time's most powerful (and dangerous) leaders, and boldly spoke the truth. Daniel would've been more straightforward in staying quiet, but great leaders don't avoid hard conversations.

- Leadership isn't about keeping people happy but helping them grow.
- Speaking up requires courage, especially when challenging someone in authority or calling out something wrong.

Silence doesn't protect people from consequences. Speaking truth in love could be the wake-up call someone needs.

2. CHOOSING HUMILITY, REGARDLESS OF THE COST

Daniel didn't take credit for his ability to interpret the dream. He knew his wisdom came from God, not himself. Similarly, Nebuchadnezzar's downfall was rooted in pride, and Daniel called him to humility.

- Humility is expensive; it will cost you your pride, opinions, and sometimes your perceived status.
- Humility says: "It's not about me."
- Authentic leadership isn't about being in the spotlight, it's about serving others and pointing them to something greater.

Are you leading from a place of pride or humility? Do you seek to build your name or God's?

3. RELEASING CONTROL OF OUTCOMES

Daniel didn't know how the king would respond to his advice, but he said what God called him to say and trusted the outcome to God. Leadership means letting go of what you can't control:

- You can't control how people respond to correction.
- You can't control every detail of your team or plans.
- But you can stay faithful to what God's called you to do.

Authentic leadership is about obedience, not outcomes.

4. BEING THANKFUL FOR YOUR CURRENT POSITION

Daniel stayed faithful in his role, even when it wasn't glamorous or easy. Nebuchadnezzar needed the reminder, too: his position and success were gifts from God, not something he earned on his own.

- Gratitude shifts your perspective, reminding you that your position is a privilege, not a right.
- Leaders who are thankful inspire others to see the good in their circumstances, too.

Are you grateful for the position God has given you, or are you focused on what's next?

5. EXTENDING MERCY

Daniel called Nebuchadnezzar to repent by "being kind to the oppressed." Mercy isn't just about withholding judgment, it's about actively stepping in to help those in need.

- Leaders extend mercy by forgiving mistakes, even when it's hard.
- Mercy also means advocating for those who don't have a voice, offering help to those in need, and creating space for second chances.

Leadership isn't just about authority, it's about compassion.

CLOSING THOUGHT:

Daniel's leadership was marked by courage, humility, faithfulness, and compassion. He didn't shy away from hard truths and trusted God with the results. When we lead like Daniel, we reflect God's heart in every situation.

PRAYER FOR LEADERS:

"God, give me the courage to speak truth, the humility to stay grounded, and the faith to release outcomes to You. Help me be thankful for where You've placed me and extend mercy to those around me. May my leadership reflect Your heart. Amen."

The Effect

- Is there a situation in your life where you need to speak up? Pray for wisdom and courage to say what needs to be said, even if it's hard.

- Take one step this week to lead with humility—admitting a mistake, giving credit to your team, or serving in an unseen way.

- What's one situation you're trying to control that you need to release to God? Write it down, pray over it, and choose to let go.

- Take five minutes today to thank God for your current position. Whether it's a role at work, school, or church, ask Him to help you lead well where you are right now.

- Who in your life needs mercy right now? Maybe it's someone you need to forgive, encourage, or help. Take one step toward showing them God's kindness this week.

Chapter 6

CLARITY *Over* CHAOS

Something shifted in our house the day my mom came home without her job. She had been let go, not because she was underperforming or causing problems, but because she held a conviction. Sunday was the Lord's day, and she refused to treat it like every other day of the week. She respectfully declined when they told her they needed her to work weekends. She stood her ground. And just like that, the job was gone.

I expected sadness. Maybe frustration. Maybe even anger at the people who let her go. But that's not what I saw.

She didn't complain. She didn't shake her fist at heaven or wallow in defeat. She did the opposite. She thanked God. Not sarcastically or reluctantly, she was genuinely thankful. Not because she had lost her income, but because she had gained time with me. Time she felt she had been missing out on. And get this, she still spoke highly of her former boss. I never heard her tear them down or tell a revenge story. She remembered the good parts of her time there and left the rest in God's hands.

While others might've spiraled into bitterness or panic, she anchored herself in clarity and gratitude. She made a list, yes, an actual handwritten list, of what she wanted in her next job. Not just vague hopes. She wrote her perfect job description, prayed over it, and kept it on the table where we could see it.

> *Contentment is a leadership superpower, it frees you to lead confidently without comparison.*

She also made a list of non-negotiables, things she wouldn't compromise on the next time. Her values weren't up for debate. She knew who she was, and that grounded her.

And it wasn't just about her breakthrough, she celebrated others too. I watched her light up when a friend got promoted or when someone landed a role they had prayed for. There wasn't a trace of jealousy in her, just pure joy.

Somehow, in the middle of joblessness, she was still giving, dropping off groceries to other families, helping friends with their resumes, and sharing words of encouragement like nothing had changed.

But everything had changed.

She showed me that real leadership starts with clarity, knowing who you are and what you stand for. And it's sustained by gratitude, being deeply, fiercely thankful even when life doesn't go the way you planned. She taught me that what you focus on expands. And she chose to focus on God's faithfulness, the time we had together, and the blessings we did have.

That season could've broken her. But it didn't. It built her. And it quietly built me too. I lead differently now because of her. I lead with conviction and a clear sense of what matters most. And when the pressure is high or something goes sideways, I remember her posture. Calm. Grateful. Certain of who she was.

SCRIPTURE FOCUS: PSALM 73:1–5

Surely God is good to Israel, to those pure in heart. But as for me, my feet had almost slipped; I had nearly lost my foothold, for I envied the arrogant when I saw the prosperity of the wicked. They have no struggles; their bodies are healthy and strong.

1. SEEING THE GOOD AROUND YOU

The psalmist starts by acknowledging that "God is good to Israel," but struggles to focus on that truth when surrounded by distractions. Leadership requires seeing the good, even when life feels unfair.

- **Gratitude shifts your perspective from envy to appreciation.**
- **Great leaders find the good in their teams, circumstances, and opportunities, even when things aren't perfect.**

Seeing the good doesn't mean we ignore challenges, it means that we focus on what God is already doing.

2. BEING SELF AWARE

The psalmist is honest about his internal struggle: "As for me, my feet had almost slipped." Leadership starts with knowing yourself, your struggles, tendencies, and areas for growth.

- **Self-awareness helps you identify envy, pride, or insecurity before they control you.**
- **Leaders who are honest about their weaknesses can grow stronger and lead others more authentically.**

Where are you struggling right now? Are there areas where comparison or envy is creeping in?

3. CELEBRATING WHERE YOU ARE AND WHAT YOU'RE DOING

It's easy to compare your journey to others and feel like you're falling behind, but leadership means celebrating the work God is doing in your life right now. The psalmist struggled with envy but ultimately realized the importance of focusing on his unique calling.

- You're not called to someone else's journey, celebrate your own.
- Recognize the purpose and value of what you're doing right now, even if it feels small.

Contentment is a leadership superpower, it frees you to lead confidently without comparison.

4. NOT MAKING ASSUMPTIONS BUT GATHERING FACTS

The psalmist assumed that the wicked lived perfect, carefree lives: "They have no struggles; their bodies are healthy and strong." But later in the chapter, he realizes he was wrong. Assumptions can cloud your leadership and distort reality.

- Leaders don't jump to conclusions, they seek clarity.
- Ask questions. Gather facts. Get perspective before making decisions.

Assumptions limit understanding; facts bring wisdom.

CLOSING THOUGHT:

Psalm 73 reminds us that leadership requires seeing clearly, the good God is doing and the areas where we need to grow. It challenges us to let go of envy, celebrate our current season, and lead with clarity instead of assumptions. When we do, we can lead with gratitude and purpose.

PRAYER FOR LEADERS:

"God, help me to see the good You're doing around me and in me. Teach me to lead with self-awareness, gratitude, and truth. Help me celebrate where I am and avoid assumptions as I seek clarity in every situation. Amen."

The Effect

- Write down three things you're thankful for right now. Spend time thanking God for His goodness in your life.

- List one thing you're proud of in your current season. Celebrate your progress instead of focusing on where you think you should be.

- Take a moment to reflect or journal: "What's one thing I need to work on to grow as a leader and follower of Christ?"

- Is there a situation where you've made assumptions without seeking clarity? Take time this week to ask questions and get the whole picture.

The **INFLUENCE** *Effect*

Chapter 7

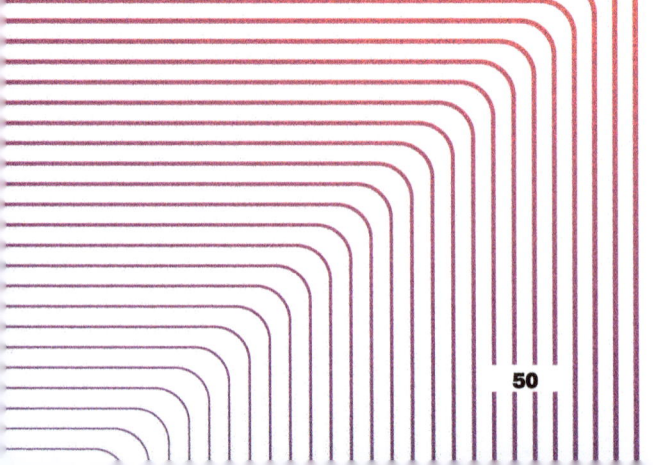

USE WHAT *You've Got.* START NOW.

A ndrew didn't wait for perfection. While some people were collecting rejection emails and polishing resumes for companies that never called back, he cracked open his iPad, pulled out his Apple Pencil, and started drawing. That was it. No budget. No fancy setup. Just a guy with a dream and a device.

He always wanted to work in animation. Not in a "that-would-be-cool" way, but the real kind. The kind that keeps you up at night thinking of characters and storyboards, the kind that makes you pause mid-conversation to jot down an idea. He applied everywhere. Sent portfolios. Reached out and got nothing but silence or polite rejections. Most people would've taken the hint. He didn't.

> *Leadership isn't about having all the answers but helping others discover them.*

Instead of waiting for someone to give him a chance, he created his own. He got on YouTube and started watching tutorials. Studied the craft. Honed his style. He'd animate small scenes, post them, get feedback, tweak them, and try again. Over and over. He didn't have a studio behind him. He had an iPad on a kitchen table. And that was enough. Fast forward, and now he's working with companies that once ignored his emails. They didn't open the door, he built one and walked through it himself. Today, business owners, creatives, and organizations bring their visions to Andrew. He turns ideas into movement, literally. He sketches what people have in their heads and brings it to life. But what I respect most about him isn't the success. His decision early on is to use what you've got. Start now, no waiting for permission.

There will be no complaining about a lack of resources, no stalling until the conditions are ideal, just movement, faith, and forward movement.

Andrew the animator did as Andrew the disciple did two millennia before he did: used what was available to him in the moment and moved forward in faith.

SCRIPTURE FOCUS: JOHN 6:8–9 (MSG)

> *One of the disciples, Andrew, brother to Simon Peter—said, 'There's a little boy here who has five barley loaves and two fish. But that's a drop in the bucket for a crowd like this.*

1. ASKING GREAT QUESTIONS TO DEVELOP THE TEAM AROUND YOU

Andrew's contribution in this moment wasn't just finding the boy with the loaves and fish, it was asking the unspoken question: "What can we do with what we have?" Great leaders don't just give answers; they ask questions that challenge their team to think creatively and grow.

- Questions like "What do you think?" or "How can we approach this?" empower others to find solutions.
- Asking the right questions helps your team see opportunities they might otherwise miss.

Takeaway: Leadership isn't about having all the answers but helping others discover them.

2. FOCUSING ON WHAT YOU DO HAVE INSTEAD OF WHAT YOU DON'T

Andrew acknowledged the small amount of food but still brought it forward. Too often, we focus on what we lack instead of leveraging what we have.

- What you have may feel small, but God can multiply it.

- Leadership means looking at your resources (time, talents, opportunities) and saying, "How can I use this to move forward?"

Are you fixating on what you're missing or focusing on what you can do with what's in your hands?

3. SPEAKING UP IN PROBLEMATIC MOMENTS

Andrew could've stayed quiet, thinking, "This won't help." Instead, he spoke up and brought the little boy's offering forward. Great leaders don't let doubt or fear keep them silent under challenging situations.

- Speak up when you see an opportunity, even if it feels small.

- Your voice and ideas might be needed to spark a solution.

Silence in moments of challenge is a missed opportunity to lead.

4. FOCUSING ON THE FIRST STEP

Andrew didn't solve the entire problem in the face of feeding thousands, but he took one step: bringing the boy to Jesus. Leadership isn't about solving everything at once but moving the mission forward one step at a time.

- **Progress often starts small. Take one step, then another.**
- **Trust that God will multiply your efforts as you move in obedience.**

What's one step you can take today to address a problem or move closer to your goal?

CLOSING THOUGHT:

Andrew's leadership reminds us that boldness, creativity, and small steps can have a huge impact when we trust God. Leadership isn't about waiting until you have all the answers or resources, it's about asking great questions, speaking up, and moving forward with what's already in your hands. Lead boldly with what you have.

PRAYER FOR LEADERS:

"God, help me ask the right questions to inspire others, focus on what I have instead of what I lack, and speak up when challenges arise. Teach me to trust You with the small steps, knowing You can multiply my efforts for Your purpose. Amen."

The Effect

- **In your next team meeting, group project, or conversation, ask a thoughtful question to draw out others' ideas instead of immediately offering a solution.**

- **Write down three things you already have—skills, relationships, or opportunities—and ask God how to use them to take a step forward.**

- **Consider a situation where you've stayed quiet but could've offered insight or help. This week, commit to speaking up when a similar opportunity arises.**

- **Instead of focusing on the entire picture, identify one actionable step you can take this week and commit to it.**

The **INFLUENCE** *Effect*

Chapter 8

STOP STALLING.
Start Stepping.

He'd been lacing up cleats since he was seven. By the time we were in high school, people didn't just know his name, they expected it to end up on an NFL roster. Coaches built offenses around him. Defenses built schemes just to slow him down. On Friday nights, he was unstoppable.

The **INFLUENCE** *Effect*

It wasn't a surprise when a Division I scholarship came in. What surprised people, though, was what he was most excited about: not the jersey, not the stadium, not the spotlight, but the degree. Football had opened the door, and he was grateful for it. He never once disrespected the game that gave him so much. But while others focused on how far he could go on the field, he started wondering how far he could go beyond it.

The bigger the crowds got, the clearer it became, football was his past, not his future.

Family. Coaches. Friends. Everyone had an opinion. Most said, "You've got a shot, don't waste it. Make it to the league."

But he saw something different. In football, he saw memories. In business, he saw potential. And here's what separates him from most people: he knew when to move on and didn't wait until it was too late. He didn't walk away out of frustration or failure. He walked away because he felt something bigger calling. He didn't rush it, but he didn't stall either. He made a choice, clear, deliberate, and full of faith.

Scripture records a similar situation in Deuteronomy:

DEUTERONOMY 1:6–8

The Lord our God said to us at Horeb, 'You have stayed long enough at this mountain. Break camp and advance into the hill country… See, I have given you this land. Go in and take possession of the land the Lord swore he would give to your fathers, to Abraham, Isaac, and Jacob, and their descendants after them.

Here we see God giving the Israelites similar instructions: move confidently into the future, not as a result of who they were but as a result of the Lord's promise to them. Fast forward to today, our friend the football player owns a medical device company that helps people across the country live longer, healthier lives. And he still carries the lessons of the game with him, discipline, resilience, grit, but he's using them on a different field now.

When I think about his story, I think about how hard it is to leave something that works. Something you're good at. Something everyone else believes you should stick with. But great leaders don't just do what makes sense to everyone else, they do what's right for where they're going. He taught me that you can honor your past while moving forward into your future. Knowing when to walk away isn't a weakness, it's wisdom.

It takes courage to step into something new. It takes even more to let go of something that once defined you. But that's what real leadership looks like, not staying stuck, but moving forward with purpose, faith, and vision.

1. KNOWING WHEN TO MOVE ON TO FRESH IDEAS

God told the Israelites, "You have stayed long enough at this mountain." Leadership often means recognizing when to let go of the familiar and step into something new. Staying too long physically, mentally, or spiritually in one place can hold you back from growth.

- **Fresh ideas require boldness to leave behind what's comfortable.**

- Great leaders ask: "Is this still working, or is it time for a change?"

While staying in the same place too long may feel safe, it can limit the new opportunities God has for you.

2. TAKING THE NEXT STEP THAT WILL LEAD TO A GREAT OPPORTUNITY

God didn't just tell the Israelites to leave; He pointed them toward the next step: "Go in and take possession of the land." Leadership means identifying and taking intentional steps toward your goals, even small ones.

- Don't wait for everything to be perfect, move forward with what you have.
- The next step may not look glamorous, but it will open the door to more significant opportunities.

What's one step you can take today toward the vision or calling God has placed in your heart?

3. REMEMBERING WHERE YOU'VE BEEN SO YOU CAN HAVE FAITH FOR WHAT'S NEXT

God reminded the Israelites of His promises and their history: "See, I have given you this land." Reflecting on where you've been, challenges and victories, builds your faith for the future.

- Remember God's faithfulness in the past to trust Him for what's ahead.
- Leaders use the lessons of the past to inspire confidence for the next step.

Looking back isn't about staying stuck, it's about gaining perspective and faith in what's next.

CLOSING THOUGHT:

Deuteronomy 1 reminds us that leadership is about movement, knowing when to move on, taking the next step with courage, and trusting God for what's ahead. Great leaders don't stay stuck; they move forward with purpose, faith, and vision.

PRAYER FOR LEADERS:

"God, help me recognize when to step into something new. Give me the courage to take the next step and the faith to trust You based on what You've already done. Lead me boldly into the opportunities You've prepared for me. Amen."

The Effect

- **Evaluate one area of your life (a habit, routine, or mindset). Ask yourself: "Is it time to move on or try something new?"**

- **Write down one action step you will take this week to move closer to your goal, then commit to it.**

- **Reflect on a moment when God came through for you. Write it down and thank Him for His faithfulness. Use it as motivation to trust Him with your future steps.**

Chapter 9

DON'T JUST *Build It.* OWN IT.

He could've justified it. The numbers weren't far off. Nothing dramatic. There were a few adjustments and tweaks tucked away in a spreadsheet that no one outside the building would ever see. That's what his boss was asking for. Quiet pressure wrapped in corporate language. "We just need to tighten this up." "The board will

The **INFLUENCE** *Effect*

appreciate the savings." "It's not illegal, it's strategic." But he knew better. He'd spent the last decade building a reputation for precision. Clean books. Honest margins. No shortcuts.

But now, in a leadership position, it wasn't just about him anymore. Newer hires were watching. Smart. Sharp. Eager. Young professionals looked to him as a model for how to lead in the real world. And he realized, this wasn't just a budget decision.

> *Longevity in leadership is built through patience and a commitment to the process.*

It was a legacy decision. So, he made the call. He pushed the spreadsheet back across the table, respectfully disagreed, and told his supervisor he wouldn't cut corners. He'd complete the budget fully, honestly, and with excellence. It wasn't easy.

There was tension. Awkward meetings. A few closed-door conversations that felt heavier than they should've. But when he turned in the final numbers, they were accurate. Fully transparent. And done without compromise. Why? Because he wasn't just crunching numbers, he was casting vision. He wanted the team under him to know that excellence still mattered. You don't sacrifice integrity for approval, but when faced with a moment where doing the right thing costs you comfort, you do the right thing anyway. And the crazy part? His team noticed. They didn't say much at first, but something shifted. Respect grew, and he raised the team's standards. They knew that this was what it looked like to lead well. That man didn't give a TED Talk. He didn't write a leadership book. He just made a hard decision when no one was cheering.

> **SCRIPTURE FOCUS: DANIEL 1:3–5**
>
> *Then the king ordered Ashpenaz, chief of his court officials, to bring into the king's service some of the Israelites from the royal family and the nobility, young men without any physical defect, handsome, showing aptitude for every kind of learning, well informed, quick to understand, and qualified to serve in the king's palace. He was to teach them the language and literature of the Babylonians.*

1. SURROUNDING YOURSELF WITH TOP TALENT

The king chose the best and brightest from Israel to serve in his palace. Leadership means recognizing that you can't succeed alone, you need to surround yourself with people who bring diverse strengths and talents.

- **Great leaders don't fear others' strengths; they leverage them.**
- **Build a team that inspires you to grow and challenges you to think differently.**

The people you surround yourself with will shape your leadership and future.

2. CHOOSING A HEALTHY LIFESTYLE

Daniel and his friends later chose a diet that honored God and kept them physically strong. Leadership requires intentional choices about caring for oneself physically, mentally, and spiritually.

- Healthy habits like eating well, exercising, and resting prepare you to lead with energy and focus.
- Your physical health impacts your ability to think clearly and serve effectively.

Are your daily habits helping or hindering your ability to lead well?

3. A COMMITMENT TO SELF, GROWTH AND DEVELOPMENT

The king's plan included educating these young men in the language and literature of Babylon. Leadership means committing to lifelong learning and growth.

- Great leaders are readers, learners, and listeners.
- Growth isn't just about knowledge, it's about applying what you learn to become a better leader.

Leaders who stop learning will eventually stop leading.

4. TEACHING PEOPLE HOW TO COMMUNICATE FOR BETTER RESULTS

Ashpenaz was tasked with teaching these young men the language and literature of Babylon. Leadership includes equipping others to communicate clearly and effectively to succeed.

- Clear communication leads to better results, stronger teams, and less confusion.
- Teach others how to share ideas, resolve conflicts, and present themselves confidently.

Are you helping the people around you communicate in ways that bring clarity and success?

5. LONGEVITY IN TRAINING

The king didn't rush the process, he planned for three years of training before these young men were ready to serve. Leadership requires patience and commitment to long-term development for yourself and others.

- Growth takes time, don't rush the process.
- Invest in others consistently, knowing that lasting impact comes through steady, intentional development.

Longevity in leadership is built through patience and a commitment to the process.

CLOSING THOUGHT:

Daniel 1 reminds us that leadership requires intentionality, surrounding yourself with great people, committing to growth, and investing in others. When you lead with vision, health, and patience, you set yourself and those around you up for lasting success.

PRAYER FOR LEADERS:

"God, help me surround myself with people who inspire me, care for my health so I can serve well, and stay committed to growing as a leader. Teach me to communicate clearly and invest in others for the long haul. May my leadership reflect Your excellence. Amen."

The Effect

- Identify one person in your life who inspires or challenges you to grow. Spend time with them this week and learn from their strengths.

- Take one step this week to improve your health, whether drinking more water, exercising, or getting better sleep.

- Choose one area where you want to grow—spiritually, emotionally, or professionally. Start by listening to a podcast or asking a mentor for advice.

- This week, help someone refine their communication by practicing presenting an idea, preparing for a conversation, or resolving a conflict.

- Think about someone you're mentoring or leading. What's one way you can invest in their growth this week?

Chapter 10

SHOW UP LIKE *Like It Matters,* BECAUSE IT DOES.

Anaya had the stats. No doubt about it. She was one of the top recruits in the country; fast, strong, explosive. The kind of athlete every program dreams about. But talent wasn't the issue. Everything else was. The transition hit her hard. She'd never been that far from family. The structure felt suffocating. Practices turned into power struggles. Team huddles felt like a battle

The **INFLUENCE** *Effect*

line. She didn't just push back, she fought. On the field, in the locker room, and meetings. It wasn't long before the conversations within the coaching staff began.

Whispers about "sending a message."

"Maybe this isn't the right fit."

"Let her go before she pulls the whole team down."

But the coach didn't budge. She didn't excuse Anaya's behavior. She didn't lower the standard for her; instead, she stayed close. Anaya's coach showed up to early lifts and asked better questions. She listened when others were quick to shut Anaya down. She made sure she knew, "You're more than your mistakes. But I won't let those mistakes de-

> *Leadership rooted in care and connection builds deeper trust and stronger relationships.*

fine you." She gave Anaya structure, but wrapped it in care. She could've walked away from Anaya or passed the problem to someone else. Instead, she chose to be present not just in games, but in the messy middle.

Not just when the player succeeded, but when she stumbled. Three years later, that same player, once written off by most, was an All-American. Disciplined. Focused. Respected.

And here's the full-circle part:

She came back to coach under the same woman who never gave up on her. That kind of leadership isn't flashy. There's no stat line for presence. No press conference for care. But it's what changes people. Great leaders don't just build programs; they build people up.

They don't just react, they remain.

They don't just correct, they connect.

They don't just lead from the front, they sit with people until they're ready to rise.

SCRIPTURE FOCUS: ESTHER 2:11

Every day, Mordecai walked back and forth near the harem's courtyard to find out how Esther was and what was happening to her.

1. REINFORCED IN ROUTINE

Mordecai didn't check on Esther occasionally, he showed up every day. Leadership isn't about one-time actions; it's about consistently showing up, even when it's not convenient or glamorous.

- **Routines build trust. When you're consistent, people know they can rely on you.**
- **Small, daily acts of faithfulness create long-term impact.**

Great leaders don't just show up when it's easy, they show up daily.

2. GOING TOWARDS OTHERS INSTEAD OF EXPECTING THEM TO COME TO YOU

Mordecai didn't wait for Esther to come to him; he went to her. Leadership means taking the initiative, seeking out others, checking in, and meeting them where they are.

- Leaders don't wait for people to ask for help—they offer it proactively.
- Moving toward others shows you care and value their well-being.

Are you waiting for people to come to you, or are you taking steps to connect with them?

3. CARING MORE ABOUT WHO PEOPLE ARE THAN WHAT THEY DO

Mordecai didn't check on Esther because of her role or accomplishments, he cared about her. Leadership isn't just about results or performance; it's about valuing people for who they are.

- People thrive when they feel seen and valued for more than they can produce.
- Leadership rooted in care and connection builds deeper trust and stronger relationships.

Great leaders focus on the heart, not just the hustle.

CLOSING THOUGHT:

Mordecai's leadership reminds us that outstanding leadership is built on consistency, initiative, and care. Because Mordecai's leadership was consistent, when he asked Esther to do something difficult, she didn't hesitate. When we show up daily, move toward others, and value them for who they are, we reflect God's heart and create a lasting impact.

PRAYER FOR LEADERS:

"God, help me lead with consistency, initiative, and compassion. Teach me to show up daily, meet others where they are, and care for them as You do. May my leadership reflect Your love and faithfulness. Amen."

The Effect

- **Identify one small, consistent action you can take this week to support your team, family, or friends. Commit to doing it every day for a week.**

- **Reach out to someone who might need encouragement or support this week. Please send a text, make a call, or meet them where they are.**

- **This week, take time to ask someone how they're doing as a person, not just about their work or tasks. Listen with empathy and genuine care.**

Chapter 11

Grace Isn't Soft, IT'S STRONG.

I should've been fired—no question about it. I was repeatedly showing up late for my shift at the thrift store. Not five minutes late. I mean rushing in through the door, already-behind-on-everything late. Management had taken a chance on me because of a friend's recommendation, and I was blowing it. I knew better. I just wasn't doing better.

Every time I walked in late, I expected the conversation. The "We appreciate you, but…" talk.

The "Let's part ways" email. But instead, my boss pulled me aside, looked me in the eye, and said something I didn't expect: "Someone showed me grace when I didn't deserve it. And that grace is why I'm still here." She didn't let me off the hook. She wasn't soft. She just didn't give up on me. She made me stay late to make up the time. She helped me figure out why I kept falling behind. And when she realized I had no system to manage my time, she sat me down and walked me through how to build one. Not because she had to. But because she believed growth was still possible, even for people who keep stumbling through the front door.

Here's what stuck with me most:

Grace isn't about letting people slide. It's about helping people rise. She led with kindness, but she didn't lower the standard. She extended grace, and required action. That experience became a blueprint for how I'd lead later on. Most of us don't need another warning, we need someone who believes we can be better and is willing to walk with us until we get there.

SCRIPTURE FOCUS: ROMANS 2:12–13

> *For all who sin apart from the law will also perish apart from the law, and the law will judge all who sin under the law. For it is not those who hear the law who are righteous in God's sight, but those who obey the law will be declared righteous.*

1. CREATING ALLOWANCES FOR FAILURE

Romans 2 reminds us that we all fall short, but God's grace meets us in our failures. As leaders, we must create space for others to fail without fear of rejection or judgment.

- Failure is part of growth; it's where people learn resilience and wisdom.
- Great leaders balance accountability with grace, helping people learn without feeling defeated.

Leadership creates an environment where failure occurs, but it does not define people.

> *Leaders who hold others accountable consistently build trust and respect.*

2. MAKING DECISIONS WITH A COMPLETE UNDERSTANDING OF ALL THE INFORMATION

Paul's teaching highlights the importance of judgment based on truth. Leaders need to take time to understand the full context before making decisions.

- Avoid snap judgments or assumptions.
- Gather all the facts and seek wisdom from others before taking action.

Are you taking time to fully understand situations before making decisions, or are you reacting based on incomplete information?

3. HOLDING PEOPLE ACCOUNTABLE

Paul emphasizes that it's not just about hearing the law but doing it. Leaders must hold themselves and others accountable to the standards they set.

- **Accountability fosters growth and integrity.**
- **It's not about punishment but helping people reach their potential.**

Leaders who hold others accountable consistently build trust and respect.

4. LEADERSHIP IS ACTION, NOT JUST GOOD INTENTIONS

Paul's words are clear: righteousness comes from doing, not just knowing or hearing. In leadership, intentions mean little without follow through.

- **People follow leaders who do what they say, not just talk about it.**
- **Action inspires others and brings vision to life.**

Are there areas where you've had good intentions but haven't followed through?

CLOSING THOUGHT:

Romans 2:12-13 reminds us that leadership requires grace for failure, intentional decision-making, accountability, and action. Great leaders don't just talk about doing the right thing, they live it out.

PRAYER FOR LEADERS

"God help me be intentional and interruptible as I lead. As I follow you, strengthen my resolve to lead with the same grace you extend to me and the integrity to uphold the weight of the position of influence you've blessed me with. Give me the strength to lead with conviction. Amen."

The Effect

- **Think about someone on your team or in your circle who may need grace for a mistake. How can you encourage them and help them grow through it?**

- **Before making your next decision, ask three questions: "What's the full story? Who can I learn from? What's the wisest course of action?"**

- **Identify one area where you need to hold someone accountable—a missed deadline, a broken promise, or a lack of follow, through. Approach the situation with clarity and kindness this week.**

- **Write down one leadership action you've been delaying and take the first step this week.**

Chapter 12

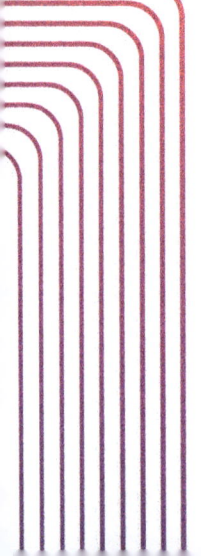

WHEN GOD *Whispers,* MOVE.

He heard from the Holy Spirit, and he moved. No committee green lit it. No investors backed it. He just got in his car, drove past miles of cornfields, stepped out onto a dusty stretch of land, and said, "This is it."

People called it crazy. They told him no one would come.

"You'll be preaching to rows of empty chairs."

"You're wasting time, money, and energy."

But he wasn't chasing logic; he was following God. So he built in the middle of nowhere. Before the highways expanded, before young families filled the zip code, before the grocery stores and the coffee shops showed up. He planted a church where no one was looking because the Spirit led him there.

No stage.

No social media buzz.

Just obedience.

> *Great leaders don't just give answers—they ask questions that inspire growth.*

He set out folding chairs. Preached to a few and prayed over empty parking lots. And kept showing up. Twenty years later, everything changed around him. That cornfield? Now a booming suburb. That empty land? Prime real estate. That tiny gathering? A church that's reached hundreds of thousands and given away millions of dollars to people in need. Families come by the thousands every weekend. Leaders are being developed. Marriages restored. Dreams awakened. And it all started because one man obeyed the voice of the Holy Spirit when everyone else called it a mistake.

SCRIPTURE FOCUS: ACTS 8:29–31

The Spirit told Philip, 'Go to that chariot and stay near it.' Then Philip ran up to the chariot and heard the man reading Isaiah the prophet. 'Do you understand what you are reading?' Philip asked. 'How can I,' he said, 'unless someone explains it to me?' So he invited Philip to come up and sit with him.

1. EMBRACING THE GUIDANCE OF THE HOLY SPIRIT

Philip didn't act impulsively; he followed the Spirit's direction to approach the Ethiopian eunuch. Leadership is about listening to God's voice and aligning with His purpose.

- Spiritual leadership begins with surrender: "What is God leading me to do?"
- Trusting the Spirit's guidance may feel uncomfortable or unexpected, but it always leads to impactful moments.

Great leaders don't just follow their instincts, they follow the Holy Spirit.

2. PURSUING WHAT TRULY MATTERS, NOT JUST ANYTHING THAT COMES ALONG

Philip didn't run to every chariot, he went to the one God directed him to. Leadership isn't about doing everything; it's about discerning what's most essential and focusing on that.

The **INFLUENCE** *Effect*

- Not every opportunity aligns with your purpose.
- Leaders must say no to distractions to fully invest in what truly matters.

Are you pursuing meaningful work, or are you simply busy?

3. LEADERSHIP IS ASKING DEEPER, MORE INSIGHTFUL QUESTIONS

Philip's first words to the eunuch weren't a sermon but a question: "Do you understand what you are reading?" Leadership is about asking questions that provoke thought, foster connection, and open doors for growth.

- Insightful questions show genuine curiosity and care.
- The right question can spark transformation and deeper understanding.

Great leaders don't just give answers, they ask questions that inspire growth.

4. BEING TRANSPARENT ABOUT WHERE SUPPORT IS NEEDED

The Ethiopian eunuch admitted his need for guidance: "How can I unless someone explains it to me?" Leaders who are honest about their limitations and ask for help create opportunities for collaboration and growth.

- **Transparency builds trust and invites others to step in with their strengths.**
- **Vulnerability isn't weakness—it's a sign of courage and humility.**

Are you willing to admit when you need help, or are you trying to do everything independently?

5. EXTENDING HEARTFELT INVITATIONS TO OTHERS

The eunuch invited Philip to join him, creating space for a meaningful conversation. Leadership means allowing others to walk alongside you, share insights, and grow together.

- **Invitations create connection and collaboration.**
- **Leaders who invite others to foster a culture of inclusion and teamwork are irreplaceable.**

Great leaders extend opportunities to others, empowering them to contribute and grow.

CLOSING THOUGHT:

Acts 8:29–31 reminds us that leadership is Spirit-led, intentional, and relational. It's about asking the right questions, inviting others into the journey, and focusing on what truly matters. When you lead this way, you create space for transformation, not just for others, but for yourself.

PRAYER FOR LEADERS:

"Holy Spirit, guide my steps as I lead. Help me focus on what matters most, ask meaningful questions, and be honest about where I need support. Teach me to invite others into what You're doing so we can grow together for Your Kingdom. Amen."

The Effect

- Spend ten minutes in prayer or reflection today, asking, "Holy Spirit, what are You guiding me to do right now?" Then, take one small step in obedience.

- Review your current commitments. Identify one task, opportunity, or activity that isn't aligned with your purpose, and consider letting it go to focus on what matters most.

- This week, practice asking one thoughtful question in your following conversations, such as, "What do you think this means?" or "How can I better support you?"

- Identify one area where you could use support and ask someone for help this week.

- This week, invite someone to join you in a project, conversation, or moment of growth. Look for ways to involve others in your work.

Chapter 13

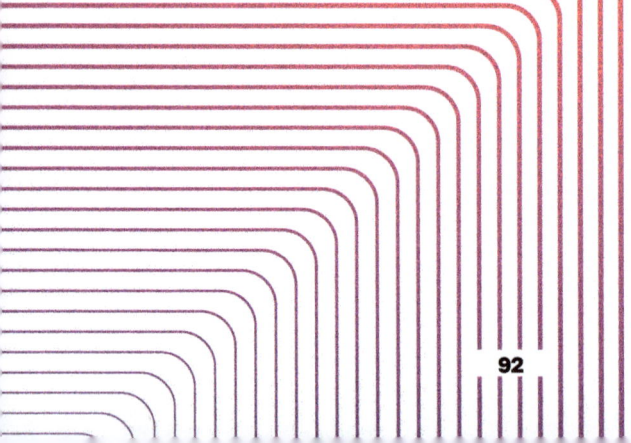

CRISIS DOES NOT WAIT, *Neither Should You.*

While most people froze, she built. Amy had spent twenty years on the factory floor, steady hours, long shifts, and the same rhythm day in and day out. She didn't hate it, but she carried something deeper down. Amy dreamed of speaking,

The **INFLUENCE** *Effect*

of writing, helping people find their voice. But life came fast, and bills needed paying. So, like many dreams, it got buried beneath responsibility. Then the world shut down when COVID hit. The factory closed its doors. Amy got sent home—same pay, no work, just time. While the world spiraled and everyone waited for answers, she got to work. She didn't binge her way through the quiet. Amy opened her laptop and started building. Keynote outlines. Book drafts. Ideas that had been sitting in notebooks for years finally got a voice. No big announcement or curated "journey" online.

Just quiet, disciplined focus. Amy used the crisis to prepare for her calling. While the world pressed pause, she pressed in. Amy doesn't stand behind a factory line today, she stands behind podiums. She's spoken to rooms she used to only dream about. Amy's not just an aspiring author, she's written and released three books that are changing lives. She didn't wait for the perfect time. She led herself through the crisis with wisdom. And now, she leads others with authority.

The truth is, the moment didn't feel ideal. It felt uncertain. Quiet. Isolating. But instead of sitting in fear, she followed wisdom.

And wisdom told her: "This is your time to prepare."

> **SCRIPTURE FOCUS: 2 KINGS 19:14–15**
>
> *Hezekiah received the letter from the messengers and read it. Then he went up to the temple of the Lord and spread it out before the Lord. And Hezekiah prayed to the Lord: 'Lord, the God of Israel, enthroned between the cherubim, You alone are God over all the kingdoms of the earth. You have made heaven and earth.*

1. DEALING WITH THE NEGATIVE FACTS OR BAD NEWS

Hezekiah didn't ignore the letter filled with threats from the enemy. He faced the lousy news head-on and brought it into God's presence. Leadership means acknowledging challenges instead of avoiding them.

- Ignoring problems doesn't make them go away, it makes them grow.
- Great leaders confront reality with clarity and courage, no matter how difficult the situation.

Leadership isn't about pretending challenging news doesn't exist, it's about addressing it with wisdom and faith.

> *Reacting is emotional and impulsive; responding is thoughtful and purposeful.*

2. RESPONDING, NOT REACTING

Hezekiah didn't panic or lash out when he received the threatening letter. Instead, he responded with intentionality by bringing the matter to God. Reacting is emotional and impulsive; responding is thoughtful and purposeful.

- Reacting focuses on how you feel.
- Responding focuses on what's needed.

How do you typically handle stressful or adverse situations, do you react emotionally or respond thoughtfully?

3. KNOWING WHO TO ASK FOR HELP

Hezekiah didn't try to solve the problem on his own. He immediately turned to God, the ultimate source of wisdom and strength. Great leaders know when and where to seek help.

- Pride says, "I can handle this on my own."
- Wisdom says, "I need guidance from someone stronger, wiser, or more experienced."

Leadership isn't about doing everything yourself, it's about recognizing when you need help and asking the right person.

CLOSING THOUGHT:

2 Kings 19:14–15 shows us that leadership in challenging moments requires courage, intentionality, and humility. By addressing the problem, responding thoughtfully, and seeking help, Hezekiah modeled how to lead through a crisis with faith and wisdom.

PRAYER FOR LEADERS:

"God, help me face challenges with courage, respond with wisdom, and seek the right help when needed. Teach me to trust You in every situation and lead with faith and purpose, even in difficult times. Amen."

The Effect

- **Think of a challenge or tough situation you've been avoiding. Take one step today to face it, whether having a conversation, seeking advice, or praying over it.**

- **The next time you face lousy news, pause and ask yourself: "What's the best way to respond to this situation?" Take a moment to pray or reflect before acting.**

- **Think of a situation where you feel stuck. Identify someone you trust—a mentor, a friend, or God—and seek advice or support.**

Chapter 14

PURPOSE
Doesn't Flinch

At 18, I sat in a hospital chair, hooked up to chemo, trying to wrap my mind around the word lymphoma. It didn't feel real, not at that age, not with that much life ahead of me. I was told I'd need six treatments. Manageable and temporary, they said, and I held on to that.

The **INFLUENCE** *Effect*

What changed me wasn't the diagnosis; it was the man sitting across the room. He'd been coming to that same infusion room for years, you read that right, years. Every day, same chair, same routine, same quiet fight. One day, I finally asked him how he kept showing up with that kind of peace. He didn't hesitate. He said, "I don't see things as they are. I see them as they should be." That one sentence rearranged something in me.

He could've been bitter; no one would've blamed him. Instead, he carried out his purpose as if it were part of his treatment plan. He told me his goal was simple: make every person in that hospital smile. Every nurse, every patient, every scared kid in a waiting room, he saw them, spoke to them, joked with them, lifted them. And it wasn't random. He had vision. He said, "My future is set. But that doesn't mean I can't create something better for those who come after me." So he built a community right there in the chemo ward. He brought in cards, conversation, and hope. He turned his pain into a mission. I walked into that building focused on survival. But I walked out of it with a blueprint for purpose-driven leadership.

SCRIPTURE FOCUS: PSALM 139:13–16

For You created my inmost being; You knit me together in my mother's womb. I praise You because I am fearfully and wonderfully made; Your works are wonderful; I know that full well. My frame was not hidden from You when I was made in the secret place and woven together in the depths of the earth. Your eyes saw my unformed body; all the days ordained for me were written in Your book before one of them came to be.

1. HAVING A STRONG SENSE OF IDENTITY AND PURPOSE

The psalmist celebrates God's intentional creation of him with value and purpose. Leadership begins with understanding who God made you to be and fully embracing that identity.

- Knowing your identity gives you the confidence to lead authentically.
- When you lead purposefully, you inspire others to discover their own.

God created you intentionally, and your leadership reflects God's unique design for your life.

2. BELIEVING IN YOUR POTENTIAL AND THE POTENTIAL OF THE PEOPLE AROUND YOU

Psalm 139 reminds us that we are "fearfully and wonderfully made." As a leader, it's essential to see both your potential and the gifts in others.

- Believe in your ability to grow and improve, even when it's hard.
- Encourage and call out the gifts and strengths in those you lead.

Reflection: Do you focus more on limitations or possibilities, in yourself and others?

3. EXPECTING GREAT RESULTS FOR THE FUTURE

The psalmist declares that all his days were written in God's book before they came to be. This passage speaks to God's sovereignty and good plans for the future. Great leaders share this perspective of hope and expectation.

- Expectation is contagious; others are inspired to pursue it with you when you believe in a better future.
- Leadership means helping others see what's possible, even when circumstances seem uncertain.

Leadership isn't just about reacting to the present, it's about envisioning a better future and taking steps toward it.

CLOSING THOUGHT:

Psalm 139:13–16 reminds us that we are uniquely designed for a purpose, full of potential, and called to expect great things in the future. When we lead with this mindset, we inspire others to embrace their identity, believe in their potential, and walk boldly toward the future God has planned.

PRAYER FOR LEADERS:

"Thank you for creating me with purpose and potential. Help me lead with confidence, see the gifts in others, and inspire hope for the future.

Teach me to trust in Your plans and take bold steps forward in faith. Amen."

The Effect

- **This week, reflect on your God, given strengths and purpose. Write down one way you can use them to lead more confidently.**

- **Identify someone in your life who might not see their full potential. Please encourage them by pointing out a specific strength or quality they may not recognize.**

- **Think about a goal or vision you have for the future. Write down the text, then outline three steps to accomplish it. Finally, share your plan with a trusted friend.**

Chapter 15

Lead With Heart, NOT A MASK.

She was only four, but she saw right through me. I didn't say much; I didn't want to worry her, but sickness doesn't hide well. It shifts the atmosphere, and somehow, she felt it. She walked in slowly, looked me over like she was trying to locate the pain, then climbed beside me and said, "Daddy… I'm gonna pray."

The **INFLUENCE** *Effect*

She says she's not good at praying. She stumbles through words, forgets what comes next, and sometimes mixes up Bible stories. But that day, she didn't hold back. She pushed past the nerves and prayed the most honest prayer I've ever heard, no big words. No performance. Just raw love and a heart that wanted to help. She didn't wait for someone else to fix it, she did what she could with what she had. Her words didn't heal my body but shifted something profound in my soul. In that moment, she led me, with compassion and courage. She didn't ask for permission. She didn't wait for the perfect opportunity. She just saw a need and stepped into it. And that's what real leadership looks like.

SCRIPTURE FOCUS: LUKE 14:1–5

One Sabbath, when Jesus went to eat in the house of a prominent Pharisee, He was being carefully watched. There in front of Him was a man suffering from abnormal swelling of his body. Jesus asked the Pharisees

> *Great leaders engage with the influential to shape systems and culture while serving those in need with humility and compassion.*

and experts in the law, 'Is it lawful to heal on the Sabbath or not?' But they remained silent. So, taking hold of the man, He healed him and sent him on his way. Then He asked them, 'If one of you has a child or an ox that falls into a well on the Sabbath day, will you not immediately pull it out?

1. IMPACTING THE PROMINENT AND THE POOR

In this scene, Jesus is dining with influential Pharisees while also addressing the needs of a suffering man. Leadership means recognizing that influence isn't limited to one group or another, it spans both the powerful and the overlooked.

- **Great leaders engage with the influential to shape systems and culture while serving those in need with humility and compassion.**
- **True leadership bridges the gap between privilege and pain.**

Leadership is about using your position to make an impact, whether you're speaking to the room's leaders or lifting up the overlooked.

2. ALLOWING YOURSELF TO BE INTERRUPTED

Jesus didn't ignore the suffering man because it wasn't "part of the plan." He paused, engaged, and acted. Leaders often face interruptions, and how they respond reveals their priorities.

- Flexibility allows you to address immediate needs without losing sight of long-term goals.
- Leadership is about valuing people over schedules and plans.

Are the interruptions in your day inconveniences or opportunities to serve and lead?

3. CHALLENGING PREVIOUS BELIEFS

Jesus confronted the Pharisees' rigid interpretation of the Sabbath, challenging their unwillingness to prioritize mercy over rules. Leadership means questioning outdated or ineffective systems and beliefs to make room for growth.

- Growth happens when we examine what's not working and seek better ways to move forward.
- Leaders must challenge assumptions, even when it's uncomfortable or unpopular.

Great leaders don't settle for the status quo, they ask hard questions and lead others toward healthier perspectives.

CLOSING THOUGHT:

Luke 14:1–5 reminds us that leadership involves engaging the prominent and the overlooked, being flexible enough to respond to unexpected moments, and courageously challenging unhelpful beliefs. We create space for transformation and healing by leading with compassion and boldness.

PRAYER FOR LEADERS:

"God, help me lead with compassion and courage. Teach me to impact people from all walks of life, embrace interruptions as opportunities, and challenge outdated beliefs with grace and wisdom. May my leadership reflect Your love and truth in every situation. Amen."

The Effect

- Identify someone in a position of influence and someone in need. Think about how you can encourage or support both people this week.

- The next time you're interrupted this week, pause and ask, "How can I use this moment to make a difference?"

- Reflect on a belief-system or habit you've been holding onto. Ask yourself: "Is this still helpful, or is it time to let it go?"

Chapter 16

DON'T FAKE *Integrity*— BUILD IT.

My first manager hired me at Burger King when I had no experience, no résumé worth reading, just a little confidence and a willingness to work. From day one, he taught me what I needed to do to keep the job: show up, stay sharp, keep the line moving. But what set him apart was the way he used every shift as a chance to shape something deeper.

While we dropped fries or cleaned counters, he'd ask questions that caught me off guard, like "Who are you becoming?" or "What do you want your name to mean when you're not in the room?" At first, I didn't know how to respond. Most managers stick to schedules and sidework, but he seemed more focused on the man I was becoming.

One day, I finally asked him why he asked questions like that. He looked at me and said, "Because you're a leader, and it's not just my job to help you work, it's to help you become." He could laugh and talk about the weather, but didn't waste conversations. He wanted me to carry something more profound, because he did. He led with thoroughness, honesty, and quiet integrity that didn't need to be announced. You just felt it in how he worked, spoke, and lived. I learned more about leadership in that apron than in most boardrooms. And the wildest part? Some of the values I carry into rooms worldwide started at a register, on a shift, in the back of a Burger King, because one man cared enough to lead with depth.

SCRIPTURE FOCUS: ISAIAH 29:13

> *The Lord says: 'These people come near to me with their mouth and honor me with their lips, but their hearts are far from me. Their worship of me is based on merely human rules they have been taught.*

1. NOT GIVING EMPTY PRAISE

In Isaiah 29:13, God critiques those who offer surface-level worship without authentic heart engagement. Similarly, as leaders, words of encouragement or praise must be genuine, not superficial.

- Authenticity in leadership builds trust; empty words erode it.
- Praise should be thoughtful, specific, and tied to actual effort or outcomes.

Empty words may sound good, but they don't inspire real growth. Genuine praise empowers and uplifts.

2. DEEPLY THINKING ABOUT SITUATIONS AND SCENARIOS

Isaiah warns against mindlessly following rules without understanding their purpose. Leadership requires pausing to think deeply about why things are done a certain way and how they could be done better.

- Superficial thinking leads to shallow decisions.
- Thoughtful leadership involves considering multiple perspectives, asking questions, and anticipating outcomes.

Are you making decisions based on routine or sincerely evaluating the situation?

3. SIMPLIFYING PROCESSES

God critiques worship that's bogged down by human rules and complexity. Leadership is about removing unnecessary complications to focus on what truly matters.

- **Simplicity allows teams and individuals to focus on impact rather than bureaucracy.**
- **Leaders who simplify processes create clarity and remove barriers to progress.**

Simplicity isn't about doing less; it's about doing what matters most, with greater clarity and focus.

CLOSING THOUGHT:

Isaiah 29:13 reminds us that leadership must come from a place of authenticity, intentionality, and clarity. By avoiding empty praise, thinking deeply, and simplifying processes, we can create an environment where people thrive and progress is meaningful.

PRAYER FOR LEADERS:

"God, help me lead with authenticity and wisdom. Teach me to give genuine praise, think deeply about my situations, and simplify what's unnecessary. May my leadership reflect integrity and clarity, pointing others toward what truly matters. Amen."

The Effect

- Reflect on how you give feedback or praise. This week, focus on offering one specific and meaningful affirmation to someone who deserves it.

- Identify one situation or process in your leadership where you've relied on "default" thinking. Take time this week to analyze it from a fresh perspective and see if there's a better approach.

- Look at one system, process, or habit in your leadership context that feels overly complicated. How can you simplify it to make it more effective?

The **INFLUENCE** *Effect*

Chapter 17

Cut Through
THE NOISE.

H is son plays like he has something to prove, and he does most days. Not to the other team, but to the voice in his head. He's crazy competitive, the kind of kid who'll invent stories about what someone supposedly said to fire himself up. Stuff that isn't just made up, it's intense.

"He said I talk like a baby."

"He made fun of my mom."

"They're laughing at how I stutter."

Most people on the sidelines can't tell what's real and what's a self-manufactured insult, but his dad, my friend, always knows. He doesn't explode or shut it down. He kneels beside his son, listens carefully, and speaks straight to his heart. He knows when his boy is hurting and when he's just hyping himself up in the wrong way. He doesn't just correct him; he coaches him. With love, not just logic. With discernment, not just discipline. He tells him, "You don't have to make enemies to find motivation," and then reminds him where his real strength comes from.

I've watched him do it repeatedly, turning emotional chaos into clarity, frustration into fuel. That kid walks off the court better not just as a player, but as a young man, because his dad doesn't just lead with authority, he leads with love and discernment. That's the kind of leadership that sticks, the kind that doesn't just win the game, it shapes the person.

> *Effective leaders know when to challenge and when to comfort, creating a balance that inspires trust and growth.*

SCRIPTURE FOCUS: JUDE 1:20–23

"But you, dear friends, by building yourselves up in your most holy faith and praying in the Holy Spirit, keep yourselves in God's love as you wait for the mercy of our Lord Jesus Christ to bring you to eternal life. Be merciful to those who doubt; save others by snatching them from the fire; to others show mercy, mixed with fear—hating even the clothing stained by corrupted flesh."

1. INVESTING IN YOURSELF

Jude calls believers to "build yourselves up in your most holy faith." As a leader, you can only pour into others when you're spiritually, emotionally, and mentally healthy.

- **Investing in yourself is not selfish; it's necessary for effective leadership.**
- **Spiritual growth, skill development, and self, care are vital to lead with strength and clarity.**

You can't lead others well if you neglect your growth. Strong leadership starts with a strong foundation in God and self awareness.

2. OPERATING FROM A PLACE OF LOVE

Jude urges readers to "keep yourselves in God's love." Leadership rooted in love prioritizes compassion, empathy, and a genuine desire to see others thrive.

- Love motivates leaders to serve others selflessly, without seeking personal gain.
- Leading with love also means addressing challenges with kindness and seeking restoration rather than division.

Are your leadership actions and decisions rooted in love for God and others, or do other motives drive them?

3. LEADERSHIP IS KNOWING WHEN TO BE TOUGH AND WHEN TO BE TENDER

Jude highlights the balance of leadership: "Be merciful to those who doubt… save others by snatching them from the fire." Leaders must discern when to extend gentleness and when to act with firm resolve.

- Tough leadership is about taking decisive action to protect or guide, even when uncomfortable.
- Tender leadership involves showing patience and mercy to those struggling or doubting.

Effective leaders know when to challenge and when to comfort, creating a balance that inspires trust and growth.

CLOSING THOUGHT:

Jude 1:20–23 reminds us that leadership requires intentional growth, love, driven actions, and discernment to balance toughness and tenderness. When we invest in ourselves, operate from love, and lead with wisdom, we reflect God's heart and inspire those around us.

PRAYER FOR LEADERS:

"God, help me to lead with wisdom and grace. Teach me to invest in my growth, operate from a place of love, and discern when to be tough or tender. May my leadership reflect Your character in every situation. Amen."

The Effect

- **Identify an area of your life where you need to invest more (e.g., prayer, learning, rest). Commit to taking one intentional step this week to strengthen that area.**

- **This week, make a conscious effort to approach every leadership decision with love at the center. Ask yourself, "How can I show care and compassion now?"**

- **Reflect on your leadership style. Are you leaning too much toward toughness or tenderness? Identify one relationship or situation where you need to adjust your approach.**

Chapter 18

SEE IT *Before They* BELIEVE IT

My friend bought a house that looked like it had given up on itself; broken windows, collapsing porch, a yard that hadn't seen sunlight in years. We all saw a dump. He saw a future. The price tag was laughably low; even the seller joked that he was doing my friend a disservice by selling it. But my friend didn't flinch. He didn't buy the house for what it was, he bought it for what it could become.

While the rest of us shook our heads and said we'd never put that kind of work into a place like that, he rolled up his sleeves and went to war with every crack, stain, and forgotten corner. He patched, rebuilt, painted, scrubbed, and restored, one project at a time, never losing sight of what it could be. Two years later, we walked through the front door of a house none of us recognized. The same house people once mocked is now the place everyone wishes they had—warm, open, full of character. It didn't happen by luck. It happened because someone believed in something before anyone else could see it. That's what vision does. And when you pair it with a belief that doesn't quit, you don't just renovate houses, you lead movements.

SCRIPTURE FOCUS: MATTHEW 8:13

Then Jesus said to the centurion, 'Go! Let it be done just as you believed it would.' And his servant was healed at that moment.

1. SEEING BEYOND PEOPLE'S POSITIONS OR TITLES TO SEEING THEIR REAL NEED

The centurion was an authority figure, yet he came to Jesus on behalf of his servant. Jesus didn't focus on the centurion's status but responded to his faith and the need he presented. Leadership requires looking past outward appearances or positions to see the actual needs of the people you lead.

- Leaders who look beyond titles build trust and connection.
- Recognizing real needs allows you to lead with empathy and relevance.

Leadership means addressing the heart of the matter, not just surface-level concerns.

2. BELIEVING THINGS/PEOPLE CAN BE SOMETHING BEFORE THEY ARE

The centurion believed in Jesus' healing ability without Him being physically present. Leadership involves having faith in what can be, even before it's visible.

- Believing in people's potential inspires them to grow and achieve more.
- Seeing possibilities where others see limitations fosters innovation and progress.

Do you focus on what is missing in others or see what they could become with encouragement and support?

3. IMPROVING THE LIVES OF THE PEOPLE BELOW YOU

The centurion's request wasn't for himself, it was for the well-being of his servant. Great leaders prioritize the growth, health, and success of those they lead.

- **Leadership isn't about climbing higher but lifting others up.**

- **When you invest in others' success, you create a culture of care and support.**

True leadership focuses on making a positive difference in the lives of others.

CLOSING THOUGHT:

Matthew 8:13 reminds us that leadership is about seeing potential, believing in possibilities, and investing in the well-being of others. Following Jesus' example, we can inspire those we lead and meet their real needs with care and compassion.

PRAYER FOR LEADERS:

"God, help me to see beyond titles and positions to the true needs of the people I lead. Teach me to believe in their potential, even before they see it themselves. Give me a heart to serve and improve the lives of others, just as You have done for me. Amen."

The Effect

- Think of someone you lead or work with. Take time this week to ask them, "What do you need to thrive?" and listen deeply to their answer.

- Identify one person in your circle who might feel overlooked or undervalued. This week, affirm their potential with specific, meaningful encouragement.

- Think of someone who reports to you or depends on you. Ask yourself, "How can I improve their experience or help them grow this week?" Take one tangible step to serve their needs.

Chapter 19

CREATE
What's Missing

While most leaders would've coasted on the momentum, he leaned into creativity and took a risk. His church was already thriving, services packed, and impact growing, which is the kind of story most pastors dream about. But instead of settling, he imagined something no one in the church world had tried: he created a role called an Experience Pastor.

The **INFLUENCE** *Effect*

At the time, it sounded strange, even unnecessary. But he saw something others didn't. He noticed people slipping through the cracks, first-time guests leaving with questions, regular attendees unsure of where to go next. So he put someone in charge of solving that, not preaching or planning events, but shaping the feel of the place, the flow, and the moments in between. That person's only job was to make the experience better, clearer, and more personal. And it worked. People felt seen. Systems got smarter. Growth accelerated. What once felt like an abstract idea became a strategic move that strengthened everything. Now, years later, churches across the country have borrowed the idea. The title is common. The need is obvious. But it all started with a leader who had the courage to create something new instead of copying what already existed, a leader who knew that growth doesn't just require grit, it requires imagination.

SCRIPTURE FOCUS: PSALM 96:1–2 (MSG)

Sing God a brand-new song! Earth and everyone in it sing! Sing to God—worship God! Shout the news of His victory from sea to sea!

1. INNOVATION AND DEVELOPMENT

The psalmist calls for a "brand-new song," emphasizing fresh creativity in worship and communication. Leadership requires innovation, seeking new ways to inspire, engage, and lead effectively.

- Innovation doesn't mean abandoning what works but refining, improving, and evolving.

- Leaders stay ahead by constantly learning, experimenting, and adapting to new challenges.

Stagnation is the enemy of outstanding leadership. Always look for ways to grow and improve.

2. SHARING STORIES OF TRANSFORMATION

"Shout the news of His victory from sea to sea!" This verse highlights the power of storytelling. Transformation inspires action, and leaders who share stories of growth, success, and breakthroughs help others see what's possible.

- Stories make leadership personal and relatable.
- People connect with real-life experiences more than abstract ideas.

Are you sharing stories that inspire and build faith in others?

3. ENGAGING NEW PEOPLE

The psalmist's invitation is global, "Earth and everyone in it, sing!" Leadership isn't just about maintaining current relationships; it's about welcoming new people into the vision.

- Effective leaders create inclusive environments where new people feel valued and involved.
- Growth comes from engaging fresh voices, perspectives, and talents.

Leadership expands when you make room for new people and their contributions.

4. EXPANDING WHAT IS EFFECTIVE

Psalm 96 doesn't call for a change in who we worship but in how we do it. Effective leadership involves recognizing what's working and scaling it for a more significant impact.

- Instead of reinventing the wheel, ask: "How can we take this to the next level?"
- Strengthening what's already effective creates sustainable growth.

What's one area in your leadership that's working well? How can you expand its reach or deepen its impact?

CLOSING THOUGHT:

The psalmist is extending a challenge to us. It is a challenge to worship God more deeply and richly. As you lead and influence others, seek out innovation, creative depth, and outside inspiration not so that you may be glorified but so that your leadership will be more effective and, through it, glorify God.

PRAYER FOR LEADERS:

"God, I surrender my way of leading and ask you to show me how to lead and worship you in new ways. Bless me with new ideas, innovation, and systems so that I may lead your people well. Lord, may my worship be pleasing to you. Amen."

The Effect

- Identify one area in your leadership where things have become routine. Brainstorm a new approach, method, or idea to bring fresh energy to it this week.

- This week, intentionally share a personal or team success story highlighting transformation. Use it to encourage someone or reinforce a vision.

- This week, reach out to someone new—whether on your team, church, or social circle—and find a way to involve them in something meaningful.

- Choose something currently successful and find a way to build on it this week—refining it or reframing it to make it ever more effective.

Chapter 20

SPEAK LIKE *The Future* DEPENDS ON IT

She walked into every room like she carried sunlight in her pocket, always grounded, always joyful, never flustered, even when life gave her every reason to fall apart. I finally asked her how she did it, how she stayed so full of peace when most people were just trying to make it through the day. She smiled and

The **INFLUENCE** *Effect*

said, "It's my declarations." Before the world could speak over her every morning, she spoke over herself. Truth, identity, vision, she declared what was real in her before anything happened around her.

> *Leaders set the emotional and cultural tone for their teams, families, and organizations.*

She said, "If I influence myself first, I'll lead others better. And the direction of your life will almost always follow the direction of your words." That hit me. She wasn't waiting for a moment to feel good; she was shaping the moment with her words. She understood something most people never slow down to learn: influence starts in private, not on a platform. Direction doesn't show up by accident; it's spoken, declared, and followed, one day at a time. What she carried wasn't fake optimism; it was rooted intention. Her life didn't control her voice. Her voice shaped her life.

SCRIPTURE FOCUS: JOB 29:21-25 (MSG)

"People listened when I spoke, hung expectantly on my words. After I spoke, they'd be quiet, taking it all in. They welcomed my counsel like spring rain, drinking it all in. When I smiled at them, they could hardly believe it; their faces lit up, their troubles took wing! I was their leader, establishing

the mood, setting the pace, and directing them correctly."

1. ESTABLISHING THE MOOD

Job describes how his presence and words profoundly affected those around him. Leaders set the emotional and cultural tone for their teams, families, and organizations.

- Your energy, attitude, and words create an atmosphere of peace or tension—confidence or doubt.
- People look to leaders for cues on how to respond to challenges and opportunities.

Leadership isn't just about what you say but how you make people feel.

2. SETTING THE PACE

Job's influence wasn't just about his wisdom but his consistency. Leaders determine the speed and intensity at which a team or movement progresses.

- If you move too fast, you may leave people behind.
- If you move too slowly, you may lose your momentum.

Are you setting a sustainable pace in your leadership, or are you pushing too hard or holding back?

3. PICKING A DIRECTION

Job states, "I was their leader, directing them in the right way." Leadership is about clarity—helping people know where to go and why they should go there.

- A leader without direction creates confusion and frustration.
- People follow confidence, not uncertainty.

Effective leaders don't just react to circumstances; they proactively choose a path forward.

CLOSING THOUGHT:

Job 29:21-25 reminds us that leadership is about setting the tone, determining the pace, and providing clear direction. When we lead intentionally, we create environments where people can thrive and move forward confidently.

PRAYER FOR LEADERS:

"God, help me set a positive tone in my leadership, establish a healthy pace, and provide clear direction for those I lead. Give me wisdom to know when to slow down, when to push forward, and how to guide others effectively. Amen."

The Effect

- Pay attention to how you carry yourself this week. Are you creating a mood of confidence, encouragement, and peace? Make one intentional adjustment to set a better tone in your environment.

- Identify an area in your leadership where you need to speed up or slow down. Adjust your approach this week to create a healthier rhythm.

- This week, clearly define the next step for your team, project, or personal leadership journey and communicate it with clarity and conviction.

Chapter 21

MOVE FAST.
Trust Deep.

I told my big brother I felt restless, spread thin, doing too much, chasing too many things simultaneously. He didn't rush to fix it or hand me a step-by-step plan.

The **INFLUENCE** *Effect*

He asked one question: "What are your top five priorities?"

I rattled them off, thinking I'd proven I had it under control.

But then he leaned in and hit me with the one that changed everything:

"How many of those are part of your destiny and how many are just distractions?"

I didn't answer right away. I couldn't. That one question flipped a light on in a room I didn't even realize was dark. He told me that question was his filter to shape every decision he made about his time, focus, and energy. He trusted his gut and moved fast when something aligned with his

> *Understanding vision and purpose is essential, but real impact happens when leaders take tangible steps toward execution.*

calling. But if it didn't? He walked away. Not later, immediately. It wasn't about being ruthless; it was about being clear. He said influence requires action, but real leadership requires intuition, the ability to sense what's worth pouring yourself into and what's just noise dressed up as opportunity.

At first, his advice made things feel messier. I saw how much of my schedule had nothing to do with where I wanted to go. But over time, that framework didn't just simplify my calendar; it clarified my purpose. Every decision still isn't easy, but now I lead from a place of focus, not just movement.

It started with someone bold enough to ask me what was worth my life.

> **SCRIPTURE FOCUS: JAMES 2:14–17**
>
> *"What good is it, my brothers and sisters, if someone claims to have faith but has no deeds? Can such faith save them? Suppose a brother or sister is without clothes and daily food. If one of you says to them, 'Go in peace; keep warm and well fed,' but does nothing about their physical needs, what good is it? In the same way, if it is not accompanied by action, faith by itself is dead."*

1. ACTUALIZATION TO IMPLEMENTATION

James challenges believers to know what is right and act on it. The same is true in leadership, understanding vision and purpose is essential, but real impact happens when leaders take tangible steps toward execution.

- Awareness without action leads to stagnation.
- Leaders bridge the gap between ideas and real-world application.

Leadership isn't just about realizing what needs to be done, it's about doing it.

2. NOT WALKING AWAY UNTIL YOU'VE MADE AN IMPACT

James uses the example of someone offering empty words to someone in need. Leadership isn't about saying the right things, it's about staying in the process long enough to bring about change.

- Impactful leaders don't just show up, they follow through.
- Leadership requires a commitment beyond surface-level engagement.

Are you walking away from opportunities before making a real difference?

3. DISCERNING NONSENSE

James warns against empty words that lack substance. Leaders need to develop discernment to recognize what is meaningful and simply noise.

- Not every conversation, task, or issue deserves your attention.
- Effective leaders focus on what truly matters and avoid distractions.

Leadership requires the wisdom to distinguish between what is essential and what is just wasted energy.

CLOSING THOUGHT:

James 2:14-17 reminds us that leadership involves turning beliefs into action, committing to meaningful impact, and discerning what truly deserves our attention. When we lead with intentionality, our influence becomes real and lasting.

PRAYER FOR LEADERS:

"God, help me turn my knowledge into action, stay committed to making a real impact, and develop discernment to focus on what truly matters. Teach me to lead with conviction and purpose. Amen."

The Effect

- **Identify one leadership idea or goal you've been thinking about but haven't acted on. Take one concrete step this week to move from planning to execution.**

- **This week, choose one situation where you can be more committed—mentoring someone, completing a project, or following up on a promise.**

- **Evaluate your current commitments. Identify one thing draining time and energy without producing value, and consider letting it go or restructuring it.**

Chapter 22

GIVE FIRST.
Lead Openly.

We spent the whole afternoon splitting logs. He knew what he was doing; I didn't. I swung the axe with more heart than accuracy, missed more than I hit, and winced every time the wood didn't split clean. He didn't complain or correct me harshly. He just kept working, letting me figure it out swing by swing. By the end, the stack looked solid, clean, even—as if two pros had done it.

One of us carried the weight, but when the owner came out and said, "You guys did great," my friend jumped in without hesitation and said, "Yeah, we knocked it out together." He didn't have to say that, but he did. Later, I asked him why he gave me credit I hadn't earned, and he looked at me and said, "Any effort deserves to be seen." That moment stuck. He chose to honor the swing in a world that only celebrates the finish line. And now, as I lead others, I carry that with me. Not everyone shows up with skill, but it matters when they show up with heart. People don't just want to be useful; they want to be seen. And great leaders make sure they are.

> **SCRIPTURE FOCUS: 1 SAMUEL 30:23-24**
>
> *"David replied, 'No, my brothers, you must not do that with what the Lord has given us. He has protected us and delivered into our hands the raiding party that came against us. Who will listen to what you say? The share of the man who stayed with the supplies is to be the same as that of him who went down to the battle. All will share alike.'"*

1. OPERATING WITH GENEROSITY

David refused to hoard victory for himself or allow his men to exclude others. He recognized that leadership is about sharing success and ensuring that blessings are distributed fairly.

- **True leaders recognize that their success is a collective effort.**
- **Generosity builds trust, loyalty, and a stronger team.**

Leadership isn't about taking the most considerable portion, it's about ensuring everyone is valued and rewarded.

2. REFLECTING ON PAST ACCOMPLISHMENTS AND VICTORIES

David reminded his men that "the Lord has given us" their victory. Leaders must reflect on past successes, not just to celebrate but to acknowledge where strength and favor come from.

- Reflection builds gratitude and keeps pride in check.
- Looking back at past victories fuels confidence for future challenges.

Do you reflect on your leadership journey and acknowledge God's role in it?

3. VALUING EVERY POSITION, EVEN IF IT DOESN'T SEEM IMPORTANT

David made it clear that those who guarded the supplies were just as valuable as those who fought on the battlefield. Great leaders recognize that every role contributes to success.

- No position is too small, everyone has a part to play.
- A culture of value and respect strengthens teams and organizations.

Leadership isn't just about leading from the front—it's about ensuring that every person, regardless of their role, knows they matter.

CLOSING THOUGHT:

1 Samuel 30:23–24 reminds us that leadership is about generosity, gratitude, and valuing every contribution. When leaders operate with fairness and reflection, they create a culture of unity and shared success.

PRAYER FOR LEADERS:

"God, help me to lead with generosity, gratitude, and fairness. Teach me to reflect on past victories, value every role, and recognize the contributions of those around me. May my leadership bring unity and encouragement to those I serve. Amen."

The Effect

- **Look for an opportunity to be generous this week, whether by sharing credit, resources, or encouragement with your team.**

- **Write down three past victories—big or small—that have shaped your leadership. Take time to thank God and recognize the lessons learned from each one.**

- **Identify someone on your team, workplace, or community whose role is often overlooked. Take time this week to personally acknowledge their contribution and show appreciation.**

Chapter 23

WHEN IT'S UNCLEAR, *Don't Collapse.*

The heat pressed down as we stepped into the village in Kenya, dusty paths, makeshift tents, and the weight of survival hanging in the air. We came to listen and to help, but one woman, thin, barefoot, and worn from the fight of daily life, taught us something we didn't expect.

> *Leaders who cultivate thankfulness create resilience, even in uncertainty.*

She waved us into her tent, offered a place to sit, and began gathering the little food she had left: scraps of rice, a cracked bowl, and water she had carried for miles. We tried to refuse, but through a translator, she smiled and said, "I'm thankful you came." No complaints, no explanations, just a heart full of something more profound than circumstance. Surrounded by scarcity, she still chose generosity. Chaos swirled around her, but she led with peace. At that moment, she reminded me that gratitude doesn't wait for comfort; it moves in the middle of the mess. She didn't have much, but she had enough to be grateful. And that made all the difference.

SCRIPTURE FOCUS: ACTS 27:35

"After he said this, he took some bread and thanked God in front of them all. Then he broke it and began to eat."

1. EVEN IN LACK, REALIZING WHAT YOU DO HAVE

Paul was in a shipwreck crisis, yet he focused on what was available rather than what was missing. Leaders shift their mindset from scarcity to resourcefulness.

- **Focusing on what you lack leads to frustration; concentrating on what you have leads to action.**
- **Leadership means seeing possibilities where others see limitations.**

What you have is enough when you trust God with it.

2. BEING THANKFUL IN THE MIDDLE OF CHAOS

Paul gave thanks in a storm. He didn't wait for calm waters to express gratitude. Leaders who cultivate thankfulness create resilience, even in uncertainty.

- **Gratitude shifts the atmosphere, bringing hope and clarity in difficult times.**
- **A leader's attitude in chaos impacts how others respond.**

Are you waiting for things to be perfect before showing gratitude, or are you choosing to be thankful now?

3. NOT BEING AFRAID TO DO SOMETHING DIFFERENT THAN THE CROWD

When fear controlled everyone else on the ship, Paul led with faith. Authentic leadership means making bold choices, even when they're unpopular.

- The most straightforward path is often to follow the crowd, but the right path requires courage.
- Leaders trust conviction over conformity.

Don't be afraid to lead differently if you know it's right.

4. THINKING ABOUT EVERYONE WHEN EVERYONE IS ONLY THINKING ABOUT THEMSELVES

Paul didn't just save himself; he ensured everyone on board had what they needed. Great leaders serve and protect the well-being of others, even when self-preservation seems like the natural choice.

- Self-centered leadership leads to division; selfless leadership builds trust.
- When prioritizing others, you create a culture of unity and shared strength.

Are you making decisions that benefit just you, or are you considering the people around you?

CLOSING THOUGHT:

Acts 27:35 shows that leadership isn't about waiting for perfect conditions, it's about leading with gratitude, courage, and selflessness, no matter the circumstances. The most outstanding leaders create calm in the chaos and inspire others to do the same.

PRAYER FOR LEADERS:

"God, help me see what I have instead of what I lack. Teach me to lead with gratitude, boldness, and a heart for others, even when it's hard. May my leadership reflect Your faithfulness in every season. Amen."

The Effect

- Identify one resource, skill, or opportunity you've overlooked. Instead of dwelling on what you don't have, ask, "How can I use this to move forward?"

- Write down three things you're grateful for, even in your current challenges. Please share them with someone to encourage them as well.

- Identify one situation where you need to stand firm in your values, even unpopular ones. Take a step in boldness this week.

- Find a way to put others first this week—whether in a team, workplace, or family situation. Take an action that benefits someone else, even if it requires personal sacrifice.

Chapter 24

DON'T *Confuse Busy* WITH BUILT

Back in sixth grade, one of the kids in our class was overweight, quiet, always in the back, and couldn't do four pull-ups, the number needed to pass our fitness exam.

The rest of us didn't think twice about it, but when his turn came and he struggled on the bar, some kids laughed, and he walked out with his head down and tears in his eyes. None of us knew then that he came back again and again, after school, before most of us even got off the bus.

> *Great leaders don't quit when it's hard; they push through until the job is done.*

He didn't announce it or post about it. He just showed up, grabbed the bar, and worked. Week after week, month after month, while the rest of us forgot about the test, he locked in. By the final semester, he walked into class, stepped up, and knocked out every pull-up like he was born for it. No shortcuts. No excuses. Just grit. He didn't need a coach to hype him or a crowd to notice he needed a goal and the courage to sweat for it.

SCRIPTURE FOCUS: NEHEMIAH 4:6–9

"We kept at it, repairing and rebuilding the wall. The whole wall was soon joined together and halfway to its intended height because the people had a heart for the work."

1. BEING TENACIOUS AND CONSISTENT

Nehemiah and his team didn't stop when obstacles arose, they kept working. Leadership requires perseverance, especially when challenges threaten to derail progress.

- **Success isn't about quick wins but about staying committed through resistance.**
- **Consistency in leadership builds momentum and inspires others to keep going.**

Great leaders don't quit when it's hard; they push through until the job is done.

2. THE LEADER GETTING THEIR HANDS DIRTY

Nehemiah didn't just delegate; he worked alongside the people. Leadership isn't about sitting back, it's about demonstrating commitment through action.

- **Leaders who work with their teams earn trust and respect.**
- **Being present in the work helps leaders understand real challenges firsthand.**

Are you leading from a distance or actively engaged in the work?

3. CREATING PROGRESS REPORTS

The wall was built halfway because Nehemiah and his team tracked progress. Effective leaders don't just work, they measure success and make adjustments.

- Progress tracking keeps teams motivated and focused.
- Small wins should be acknowledged to keep momentum high.

Leaders celebrate milestones, not just the final victory.

4. LEADERSHIP IS TEACHING PEOPLE HOW TO ENJOY THEIR WORK

Nehemiah's team worked with "a heart for the work." When leaders cultivate enthusiasm and purpose, work becomes meaningful rather than draining.

- The best leaders create environments where people find joy in their efforts.
- Purposeful work leads to passion and engagement.

Are you fostering an atmosphere where people enjoy what they do, or is work seen as just an obligation?

CLOSING THOUGHT:

Nehemiah 4:6–9 teaches that leadership is about perseverance, active participation, measurable progress, and cultivating joy in the work. Leaders embody these traits and inspire others to stay committed and find purpose in their efforts.

PRAYER FOR LEADERS:

"God, help me lead with consistency, commitment, and engagement. Teach me to celebrate progress, work alongside my team, and create an environment where people enjoy their work. May my leadership reflect endurance and purpose. Amen."

The Effect

- Identify an area where you've been inconsistent. Make a plan to show up consistently for the next seven days, regardless of obstacles.

- Find a way to physically or personally participate in something you typically delegate this week. Show your team that you're willing to work alongside them.

- Identify a long, term goal you're working on. Take time this week to assess where you are, what's working, and what needs adjustment.

- This week, take time to encourage your team or peers. Find a way to make the work more engaging and meaningful.

Chapter 25

TAKE THE HEAT.
Lead Anyway.

He didn't build the business he inherited it. His dad started it from nothing, poured decades of sweat into it, and turned it into something strong. When his dad passed it down, the paperwork said he was in charge, but the reality? He never owned it.

The **INFLUENCE** *Effect*

Not really. He liked the perks. He liked the title. He liked the money. But he didn't love the work. Didn't know the customers. Didn't study the market. Didn't dream about where it could go. He just showed up, kept it afloat, and tried not to rock the boat. But a business doesn't thrive on autopilot.

While other companies took risks and evolved, he played it safe. He refused to shift. Refused to innovate. And when competition got sharper, he froze. No strategy. No fight. Just passive hope that things would turn around. They didn't. The company folded slowly, then suddenly. And the saddest part? It didn't collapse because the market moved too fast. It collapsed because he didn't move at all. What his father spent years building, he lost in just a few. Not because he was incapable, but because he thought leadership was a position instead of a responsibility. He wanted the fruit without tending the soil. Wanted the reward without the risk. And leadership doesn't work like that.

SCRIPTURE FOCUS: MATTHEW 25:24–30 (MSG)

> "The servant given one thousand said, 'Master, I know you have high standards and hate careless ways, that you demand the best and make no allowances for error. I was afraid I might disappoint you, so I found a good hiding place and secured your money. Here it is, safe and sound down to the last cent.' The master was furious: 'That's a terrible way to live! It's criminal to live cautiously like that!'"

1. STEADY STREAM OF INVESTMENT

The parable of the talents reveals that leadership is about continually investing what we've been entrusted with, skills, time, resources, or people. Growth doesn't happen from occasional effort but from consistent stewardship.

- **Leadership isn't about maintaining, it's about multiplying.**
- **Investing small but consistently leads to a more significant impact over time.**

Takeaway: The best leaders deposit effort, wisdom, and encouragement daily.

2. REFUSING TO MAKE EXCUSES

The unfaithful servant blamed fear for his lack of action. Leaders must take responsibility rather than justify inaction.

- **Excuses kill momentum and breed stagnation.**
- **The best leaders own their decisions, whether they succeed or fail.**

Reflection: Are you allowing fear or doubt to prevent you from taking on a leadership opportunity?

3. TAKING RISKS

The master commended the servants who took action with their talents, even though there was risk involved. Leadership requires faith, even when the outcome isn't guaranteed.

- **Playing it safe often leads to lost opportunities.**

- True leaders take calculated risks that stretch their capacity.

Takeaway: Bold leadership isn't reckless, it's willing to step forward when others hesitate.

4. GROWING WHAT YOU'VE BEEN GIVEN

The faithful servants in the parable didn't complain about what they started with, they focused on increasing it. Great leaders don't wish for different opportunities; they maximize what they already have.

- Complaining about what you lack keeps you from using what you have.
- Growth happens when you commit to stewarding your current resources well.

Reflection: Are you maximizing the opportunities and resources in front of you?

CLOSING THOUGHT: LEADING WITH ACTION AND ACCOUNTABILITY

Matthew 25:24–30 reminds us that leadership requires investment, personal responsibility, bold risk-taking, and faithful stewardship. Playing it safe isn't an option, leaders who grow are leaders who act.

PRAYER FOR LEADERS:

"God, help me lead with courage and wisdom. Teach me to invest consistently, take responsibility for my actions, step out in faith, and grow what You've given me. May I lead boldly and with purpose? Amen."

The Effect

- Identify one area where you can invest more—whether in personal growth, mentoring others, or improving a skill. Take one small step today.

- Identify one excuse you've been using and replace it with action this week.

- This week, take one bold step in an area you've hesitated. Make the move, start the project, or have the conversation you've been putting off.

- Instead of focusing on limitations, list three things you do have that you can use to grow today.

Chapter 26

YOUR STORY
Is Not Just Yours

I sat in the back of the room expecting another polished sermon, the kind where everything wraps up perfectly and the guy with the mic is the hero. But this pastor didn't open with wins. He opened with wreckage. He talked about where he failed, who he hurt, and how long he spent running from everything God called him to be.

The **INFLUENCE** *Effect*

And he didn't rush past it, he walked us through it all. The screw-ups. The healing. The foggy middle where he didn't know who he was becoming but kept showing up anyway.

> *People follow leaders who are transparent about their path, not just their position.*

I was young, still trying to figure out who I was and what I wanted, and that kind of honesty hit different. He didn't stand there trying to impress us, he stood there carrying scars he wasn't afraid to show. And that gave me something I didn't even know I needed permission to stop performing. I didn't need a perfect past to build a meaningful future. That day, I saw what leadership really looks like. Not someone pretending they always had it together, but someone refusing to waste what they've been through. He didn't tell his story to boost his image; he said it to build us up. And that's the kind of leader I want to be.

SCRIPTURE FOCUS: PSALM 129:1–4 (MSG)

"They've kicked me around ever since I was young—this is how Israel tells it—

They've kicked me around ever since I was young, but they never could keep me down.

Their wickedness has never prevailed.

God sticks with us; He's never left our side."

1. TELLING THE STORY OF HOW YOU GOT TO WHERE YOU ARE WITH YOUR TEAM

The psalmist reflects on past hardships, showing that resilience and faith brought them through. Great leaders don't just share success, they share the journey, including the challenges and breakthroughs that shaped them.

- Storytelling fosters trust and relatability within your team.
- Sharing your journey encourages others to persevere.

People follow leaders who are transparent about their path, not just their position.

2. TALKING ABOUT YOUR FAILURES

Psalm 129 acknowledges hardships without sugarcoating them. Strong leaders don't hide failures; they use them as teaching moments.

- Admitting failures creates a culture where growth is prioritized over perfection.
- Leaders who acknowledge mistakes show others how to handle setbacks with wisdom and resilience.

Are you willing to be open about your failures so others can learn from them?

3. TEACHING PEOPLE HOW TO THINK BEFORE AND AFTER TRAUMA

The psalmist describes enduring struggles and emphasizes that God never left their side. Leaders help people navigate challenges, not just react to them but prepare for and recover from them.

- Before trauma: Teach resilience, faith, and preparation.
- After trauma: Guide recovery, reflection, and growth.

The best leaders equip others to process difficulty in a way that leads to wisdom, not just wounds.

CLOSING THOUGHT:

Psalm 129:1–4 reminds us that leadership isn't about having a perfect past but using your journey, failures included, to help others grow. Ultimately, healing is a journey, not a destination, by sharing your story, acknowledging mistakes, and guiding people through hardship, you lead in a way that builds absolute trust and resilience.

PRAYER FOR LEADERS:

"God, help me lead with transparency and strength. Give me the courage to share my story, the wisdom to talk about my failures, and the compassion to guide others through challenges. May my leadership reflect Your faithfulness. Amen."

The Effect

- **Take time this week to share part of your leadership journey—how God has shaped you through victories and struggles.**

- **Identify one past failure that helped shape your leadership. Share the lesson you learned from it with someone who might benefit from your experience.**

- **This week, talk with someone about how to grow through challenges, not just endure them. Offer guidance on thinking through difficulties with faith and strategy.**

The **INFLUENCE** *Effect*

Chapter 27

TAKE THE HIT.
Keep Building

She knew the tension wasn't in her head. The smiles felt too staged. The feedback in meetings came with an edge. And the random invites that somehow never included her? Clearer than any memo. She didn't guess—they were trying to get her fired. Not just one or two people. Multiple. Private meetings. Slack threads she wasn't in. A full-on effort to push her out. She had the receipts. Emails. Forwarded screenshots. Whispers that made their way back to her office.

The **INFLUENCE** *Effect*

People she trusted, people she had once mentored, joined in. And she could've flipped the table. She had the authority. One HR meeting, and the mess could've been cleared in a day. But she didn't take the easy way out. Instead, she got low. Listened harder. Led smarter. Every morning, she walked into that office knowing some of the same people sitting across from her were secretly working to replace her. Still, she greeted them. Asked how their families were.

> *Leaders bend without breaking.*

Celebrated their wins. She didn't ignore the issue, she just refused to give it her energy. She put that energy into vision. Into clarity. Into building what she believed in. She didn't start performing to keep their approval. She stayed rooted in who she was and what she was called to lead. Slowly, almost quietly, the shift began. One by one, the same voices that once doubted her started asking her advice. People stopped watching for her to break and started watching how she handled pressure. And it wasn't magic. It was grit. Intentional, consistent, unshakeable grit. Her presence didn't just fill the room. It leveled it. She didn't use shame to get their attention; she used strength. She didn't need to dominate the conversation; she just kept showing up with calm confidence. Eventually, every person who tried to push her out became someone who followed her in. Not because she crushed them but because she outlasted the drama, outloved the betrayal, and outled the noise.

SCRIPTURE FOCUS: II SAMUEL 18:4

'Then the king said to them, "Whatever seems best to you I will do." So the king stood beside the gate, and all the people went out by hundreds and by thousands. '

In this passage, King David is crushed by familial and governmental challenges. His son has rebelled, and there's a moment in which his leadership is questioned. He's in the face of true adversity. He, however, responds with resilience. He neither cowers nor hides; instead, he relies on his people and team. In the end, he prevails as king, albeit a wounded one.

1. DO AS I DO, NOT AS I SAY.

Resilience typically has a positive connotation, but the reality is that resilience needs the fire of adversity to reveal itself. Effective leaders teach their team how to be resilient in the face of adversity, whether they mean to or not. Your team will mimic and magnify how you respond to difficulties and challenges.

- Embrace adversity; it will mold, teach, and root you as a leader.
- Demonstrating transparency and modeling humility in challenging times makes you a more reliable leader.

People are more apt to follow a genuine leader, notwithstanding their leader's challenges, if the leader's response is honest and transparent.

2. BEND, NOT BREAK

Problems, challenges, adversity, issues, etc, can all become complicated and convoluted instantly. However, it requires a flexible leader not only to overcome but also to expand their influence further. Being effective for a season is not enough; the goal is to be constantly growing and developing in equal measure.

- Effective leaders are willing to bend while remaining faithful to the convictions and truth that have carried them thus far.

- Procedures, protocols, and systems can all be reimagined, reworked, and made new; conviction cannot; an effective leader can tell the difference.

Commit to God, His call, His truth, and His vision; everything else is discussable and flexible. Leaders bend without breaking.

3. TEAMWORK MAKES THE DREAM WORK

Resilient leaders cannot and must not have savior complexes. Quite the opposite. Your team, whether of two or two hundred, is your team. In times of adversity, a resilient leader must be humble enough to ask for help, ideas, and fresh perspectives. You are not in it alone, and you're not the only one who can "fix it".

Working towards resolving an issue or overcoming a challenge as a team rather than alone will bring you closer and make you more effective.

CLOSING THOUGHT:

It does not matter if you face adversity as a leader, but when. The reality is that adversity comes in many iterations, but one fact remains: adversity opens the door for resilience. Lean on your God, your team, and the knowledge of who is in control. Here's a clue: it's not you, and what a relief that is.

PRAYER FOR LEADERS:

"God, I thank you because you know what challenges I face and will face as a leader. The understanding that you know it all brings me peace. Lord, help me become a resilient leader so that I may be most effective in your kingdom. May I always reflect you in every decision. Amen."

The Effect

- Am I asking for something from my team that I have not modeled? If so, will you begin to model whatever "it" might be today?

- Have you become rigid or myopic in your processes or protocols? Can you reflect and ask yourself where you can bend to usher in growth in your organization?

- Think about what "savior complex" means. Is this a struggle for you? Can you look for ways to ask your team to contribute to a challenge or issue?

Chapter 28

LEAD WHEN
No One Claps

He wasn't the loudest voice in the room, but somehow he always knew what to say. He made decisions with this steady clarity, like he had a playbook no one else could see. I worked with him long enough to catch on whenever things got messy; he'd say, "My dad used to tell me..." and then drop something that hit harder than any leadership quote I'd heard. His dad had passed, but the way he led made it feel like the man was still right there, just off to the side, speaking into every moment. He didn't guess his way through the job; he carried something deeper. And it wasn't just about memory. It was about closeness.

The **INFLUENCE** *Effect*

Before his dad died, they were tight. They talked about real stuff. They spent time. And that kind of relationship left a mark. Watching him taught me this: your leadership always reflects your most intimate relationship. If the voice in your head is grounded, wise, and rooted in love, your decisions will follow that same tone. And if you want your influence to mean something, you can't fake it; you've got to stay close to the right source.

> *Integrity in leadership means following through.*

For him, it started with his dad. For me, it begins with God. Because when His voice gets familiar, your direction stops feeling random. And people don't just follow your skill, they follow your roots.

SCRIPTURE FOCUS: GENESIS 6:18 NLT

'But I will confirm my covenant with you. So enter the boat—you and your wife and your sons and their wives.'

Noah is introduced into the biblical narrative at a time in human history when, as Moses records it in Genesis, '...the Lord was sorry he had ever made them and put them on the earth. It broke his heart. Genesis 6:6 NLT. "Them" being us, humans. In this passage, we are getting a glimpse into God's reaction to humanity's sinful nature. Most people are accustomed to this story's vacation Bible school version, which focuses on the ark and the animals. Noah built the ark, and the animals got on board in pairs. However, further study reveals that there are true and tried leadership lessons we can glean from Noah's story.

1. CLOSE FELLOWSHIP BIRTHS RADICAL TRUST

The Bible describes Noah as finding favor with the Lord and walking in close fellowship with God. This close fellowship is why God can entrust Noah with building an ark. It wasn't his incredible talent as a carpenter or inclination towards animals that qualified him; it was his close fellowship with God. Similarly, the fellowship within a team will shape the quality of the work they produce. Noah trusted God because he knew God and, as a result, could trust Him.

- How well your team knows you and each other is one of the determining factors in how much trust there is within your team.

- The level of trust in your team will determine the degree of effectiveness you will have.

- Noah could complete a project bigger than himself because he trusted God, His leader, radically; he could only do that because he was well acquainted with God.

Trust, in any context, requires fellowship, and it is a leader's responsibility to set the tone within their team.

2. THERE'S ALWAYS A BIGGER PLAN

The physical ark is not the climax of this story. God focused not on building an enormous cruise ship filled with animals. The goal was to reshape and redeem humanity, rather than destroy it.

The ark was a step in the plan, not its completion. God made sure he let Noah know there was more to his plan than the building portion.

- Leaders communicate that every step is toward achieving a bigger purpose in a season of building, creating, and establishing.

- Leaders do not become myopic or hyper-focused on one task but can see the bigger plan.

- Leading with purpose will give meaning to the tasks needed to support the big picture.

Effective leaders build thinking of a greater purpose and plan, seeing beyond the tasks, but the change it will bring.

3. KEEP YOUR WORD

The resolution of this narrative isn't just the flood, the animals, or the end of the waters, it's the promise God made never to flood the earth again. Long before the rains came, God told Noah He would confirm His covenant, and He did. Noah completed a difficult task because he trusted God would keep His word.

- Leaders who sow integrity will reap faithfulness.

- Walking alongside your team as they work toward a common goal will strengthen their engagement with the big picture.

Integrity in leadership means following through, especially when the outcome isn't obvious. Like Noah, effective leaders take the next faithful step, even when the picture isn't clear.

CLOSING THOUGHT:

Noah was 600 years old when he had to build the ark, yet the Bible singles him out as the only righteous man of his time. His leadership style reflects his most significant influence, God. Your influence and leadership will reflect your most intimate relationship, root yourself in your relationship with God.

PRAYER FOR LEADERS:

"God, I want my leadership to be influential and transformational. I know this is only possible by gladly submitting myself to your ultimate plan for my life. Help me continue to walk in a close, intimate relationship with you, so that my leadership will reflect how you lead us. Amen."

The Effect

- What can you do this week to foster relational equity amongst you and your team?

- Create opportunities for your team to become further integrated and strengthen the trust within the team.

- Communicate with your team fresh and new about the big picture and how you're all working toward a common goal.

- Look for one area of your life and leadership where you can raise the standard of integrity.

Chapter 29

STOP *Motivating* START MOVING.

Middle school football wasn't impressive. We were messy, distracted, and more focused on making each other laugh than learning the plays. Our coach could've done what most do: stand on the sideline, yell, and repeat, but he didn't. After another lazy practice, he stopped mid, drill, walked off the field, and returned with pads on.

No speech. No explanation. He threw on a helmet and lined up with us. Then, he hit. Ran. Blocked. Hustled. He didn't talk about expectations; he embodied them. Everything shifted after that. We moved faster. Complained less. Matched his energy. That day taught me something I've never forgotten: real leadership doesn't need a platform or a pep talk, it requires presence. It doesn't lean on charisma or hype; it steps in, gets dirty, and sets the tone. Decisive leaders don't wait for the room to catch up; they move first and pull everyone with them. Our coach didn't just tell us what to do, he showed us what it looked like to go all in. And we followed, not because he had a title, but because he led like he meant it.

SCRIPTURE FOCUS: JUDGES 4:8–9 NLT

Barak told her, "I will go, but only if you go with me." "Very well," she replied, "I will go with you. But you will receive no honor in this venture, for the Lord's victory over Sisera will be at the hands of a woman." So Deborah went with Barak to Kedesh.

> *Leadership does not negotiate with fear; it sacrifices to obliterate it.*

1. AIM TO CONVICT, NOT CONVINCE

Deborah's aim was not to motivate Barak's emotions so that he could face and defeat the enemy; her objective was to speak to his conviction so that he would move with purpose. Her presence propelled movement, not performance.

- **Leadership does not negotiate with fear; it sacrifices to obliterate it.**

- **Influence is not about hype or charisma but about the conviction that moves the mission forward.**

- **Leaders who speak from conviction find that it is deeply rooted in purpose, and convincing is shallow and baseless.**

Deborah's objective was not to convince Barak that the Lord would be victorious, she was sure of this. Her role in this interaction is to walk Barak through a season of fear, not debate outcomes. As a result, she aims to stir conviction in him, not convince him. Effective leaders discern when to step into the gap for others and walk alongside them in different seasons.

2. DRIVE FORWARD MOVEMENT

Although Barak was intimidated by the enemy, Deborah's main priority as the leader of the people of Israel was to defeat Sisera and get to the promised land. Scripture records Deborah on the battlefield, but Barak attacks Sisera. Her presence on the battlefield demonstrates effective leadership.

- **Leaders do not shy away from uncomfortable situations when it is driving momentum toward a goal.**

- **Delegation doesn't weaken a leader's role; it tests it. It becomes a measure** of trust, preparation, and shared ownership.

- Leaders use their influence to drive action and accomplish purpose.

Takeaway: Barak accomplished what Deborah equipped him to do, win the battle. Leaders aim to equip their team with the tools to carry out the vision confidently.

3. LEAD THE DARING

Effective leaders do more than speak about rising to the occasion; they embody it with their actions. Deborah was not the only woman engaging with the enemy in this narrative. Jael, who lacked a title of distinction, had courage in abundance. She was daring, courageous, and fearless. Scripture records Sisera's death at the hands of Jael, not Barak or Deborah.

- Confident leadership allows others to take brave, decisive, and definitive action.

- Leadership is not limited to titles, platforms, or popularity. Jael didn't need any of those to be effective and victorious.

- Leaders seek to discern when to act boldly and when to wait patiently.

Jael's silent but decisive leadership led Israel to ultimate victory. She capitalized on her location, position, and relationships. Deborah's confident leadership created space for Jael's actions.

CLOSING THOUGHT:

Decisive leadership doesn't rely on charisma, hype, or connections to achieve its goals. Instead, it speaks to deep wells of conviction to inspire.

PRAYER FOR LEADERS:

"God, I want to be courageous in my leadership like Jael and Deborah were. Help me be rooted, tuned into your spirit, and decisive. Amen."

The Effect

- Find time this week to take inventory of your convictions. Are there areas of your life where you have been convinced instead of having a deep conviction?

- What uncomfortable space can you move into to generate forward movement within your team?

- How can you create space for those on your team who are daring, bold, and courageous?

Chapter 30

LEAD LIKE
Your Lit On Fire.

I still remember the first time I said it out loud: I want to be a speaker. I did not just casually mention it or toss it in a "maybe someday" list; I said it like I meant it. I had just watched someone speak on stage, and something inside me cracked open. I wasn't drawn to the mic or the lights. I was drawn to the impact. The way words could lift people. Challenge them. Wake them up. I saw it, and something in me said, "That's what I'm supposed to do." So I told a few friends. And one of them looked at me and said, "Why would you be able to do that? No one in your family does that." Another said, "I'm not trying to be mean, man, but you're not even a good speaker." And the last one just shrugged and said, "I don't see it. That's just not you." I wish I could say their words rolled off. They didn't. They cut deep. Made me question myself. Made me shrink. For a moment, I let their doubt rearrange how I saw my future. But I didn't stay in that moment.

> *Unapologetic persistence anchored in conviction is fundamental to reliable leadership.*

I disagreed with their limitations. I didn't hand them the pen to write my story. I decided to speak anyway. To work on the craft anyway. To fail, improve, repeat. I didn't wait for permission, I chased conviction. Now, I travel around the nation doing what they said I couldn't. I help people meet Jesus. I help leaders lead better. I speak into the lives of husbands, wives, creatives, executives, athletes, and students. And every time I step on a stage, I don't carry bitterness, I have clarity. They didn't need to believe in me. I just needed to believe in the call. Conviction doesn't wait for consensus. Audacity doesn't ask for applause. And persistence doesn't flinch when critics show up early. If I had listened to them, I wouldn't be here. But I listened to God instead. And that's the only reason I get to live this life today. So say it out loud. Chase what burns in you. Don't let anyone talk you out of what God spoke into you.

> *SCRIPTURE FOCUS: 1 SAMUEL 17:34–36*
>
> 'But David persisted. "I have been taking care of my father's sheep and goats," he said. "When a lion or a bear comes to steal a lamb from the flock, I go after it with a club and rescue the lamb from its mouth. If the animal turns on me, I catch it by the jaw and club it to death. I have done this to both lions and bears, and I'll do it to this pagan Philistine, too, for he has defied the armies of the living God!'

1. PERSIST, AND THEN PERSIST SOME MORE

We meet David at a young age, and although Samuel has already anointed him to become the next king, he is still a lowly shepherd boy. And the persistence of this shepherd boy grants him an opportunity on the battlefield.

- David doesn't take no for an answer, not because he was blood thirsty, but because his conviction required this response. Leaders must remain persistent when the cause comes into conflict with their convictions.

- Bold leaders lead with courage that outpaces their credentials. David highlighted how he would use his experiences with animals to defeat Goliath, not how he met their expectations of him.

Unapologetic persistence anchored in conviction is fundamental to reliable leadership. David did not give up until he got the answer he was seeking.

2. PRACTICE AUDACITY

There is no timidity in David's request; conversely, he makes an audacious statement, "I'll do it to this pagan Philistine, too". His audacious statement comes on the heels of statements where he shares how underprepared he was for the task he was asking for. One could even argue it was arrogant, except the following statement gives us a glimpse into his heart posture: "...for he has defied the armies of the living God!". His audacity was rooted in faith and conviction, not his abilities. David didn't risk his reputation; he risked the Lord's.

- Audacity rooted in faith and not pride will yield miraculous results.

- Leaders who move with audacity, conviction, and boldness shift the atmosphere they inhabit.

David's audacious leadership broke the cycle of fear that the Israelites were in. Leaders who step out with audacity activate their team's faith.

3. BE WILLING TO STEP INTO THE ARENA

The leadership arena is not for the qualified but for the willing, and David was willing. He physically stepped onto the battlefield and eventually defeated Goliath while his brothers and counterparts feared failure. David could have died, he could've failed, but the risk of stepping onto the battlefield paid off.

- Leadership is less about power and more about presence; show up for the organization, the team, and yourself, and God will meet you there.

- Failure is possible, but not permanent; fearing failure is fruitless.

- David showed up as himself with the tools that only he could use. He didn't pretend to be a strong and mighty warrior; he showed up authentically.

Whether the arena metaphorically stands in for leadership, influence, or both, show up. David offered himself from a place of faith and conviction.

CLOSING THOUGHT:

If anybody were to bet on David, the odds were not in his favor. Yet, his victory is still studied and acclaimed to this day. David's recipe was simple, he persisted with audacious faith and showed up to the battlefield. The recipe for effective leadership is just as simple as David's.

PRAYER FOR LEADERS:

"God, I want to lead with audacity and take bold risks and chances. Jesus, I want every step I take to further root my faith in you. Go before me as I take steps of faith, I know you go before me. Amen."

The Effect

- Reflect on situations past or present where you can or could have been persistent. What held you back from persisting? How can you change it moving forward?

- How can you be audacious this week? What environment do you want to see change, and how can audacity play a part in that shift?

- What arena of life or leadership have you not shown up to yet? What is holding you back from showing up?

The **INFLUENCE** *Effect*

www.ingramcontent.com/pod-product-compliance
Lightning Source LLC
Chambersburg PA
CBHW061940130526
44582CB00040B/31